"A roller-coaster ride through Portland's radical past. Who knew that being on the losing side of just about everything could be so much fun?"

—Phil Stanford, *Portland Tribune* columnist, author of *Portland Confidential*

"Michael Munk is the Lewis and Clark of Portland's radical past, leading his readers on a voyage of discovery through a long-lost and wonderfully evocative historical terrain. I only wish The Red Guide had been around in the days when I was one of those Portland radicals. Munk writes about with such knowledge (and affection)."

—Maurice Isserman, author of *If I Had a Hammer: The Death of the Old Left and the Birth of the New Left*, and former staffer at the *Willamette Bridge* and *The Portland Scribe*

"Whoop! Whoop! I'm impressed by how many names from Portland's past have not made it into our official histories and public memorials. Some were good friends of mine. Local history is too often overlooked. Good work, Mike."

—Bud Clark, Saloon keeper, Goose Hollow Inn, and Mayor of Portland, 1985–1992

"Michael Munk did a terrific job of researching local leftist and labor struggles usually ignored by conventional historians and the commercial media."

—Gene Klare, columnist, *Northwest Labor Press*. Former reporter, *The Oregonian* and the *Portland Reporter*

"What fun it is to learn about all the ordinary places that have a not-so-ordinary history. Some will call The Portland Red Guide subversive, others will welcome it as the sweet breeze of revelation, but all will have to admit it adds a fascinating new layer to appreciation of Portland. Even those Portlanders who think they know their city's past will likely find themselves shocked by the wealth of radical Portland history related in this volume."

—Sandy Polishuk, author of *Sticking to the Union: An Oral History of the Life and Times of Julia Ruuttila*

"Going to these addresses can bring to mind what has gone before and perhaps, encourage more resistance today. I had no idea so much has happened in Portland. And reading the names of people who struggled…brought up lots of memories."

—Sandra Ford, former wife of Black Panther Party leader Kent Ford

THE PORTLAND RED GUIDE

SECOND EDITION

MICHAEL MUNK

OOLIGAN
PRESS

Library of Congress Cataloging-in-Publication Data

Munk, Michael, 1934-
The Portland red guide : sites & stories of our radical past / by Michael Munk. -- 2nd ed.

      p. cm.
Includes index.

ISBN 978-1-932010-37-4 (alk. paper)

1. Portland (Ore.)--Guidebooks. 2. Radicalism--Oregon--Portland--History. 3. Radicals--Oregon--Portland--Biography. 4. Social movements--Oregon--Portland--History. I. Title.

F884.P83M86 2011
979.5'49--dc22

                         2010048684

Cover design by Alan Dubinsky, illustrations by Icky A.
Interior design by Alan Dubinsky and Tristen Knight

Ooligan Press • Department of English
Portland State University
PO Box 751, Portland, Oregon 97215
503.725.9748 (phone); 503.725.3561 (fax)
ooligan@ooliganpress.pdx.edu
http://www.ooliganpress.pdx.edu

Printed in the United States

CONTENTS

PREFACE

The Portland Police Red Squad kept detailed surveillance records until the 1980s. Groups of all ideologies were monitored and photographed. This 1941 Communist meeting took place in downtown Portland. The numbers above the men's heads corresponded to their names, which were written on the back of the photograph. *City of Portland Archives, A2001-074.2.*

S ince the first edition of *The Portland Red Guide* was published over three years ago, the question I have been asked most often was "Why did you write it?" I answered that it grew from a childhood experience, that as my school bus took me to the eighth grade in 1947, I was impressed daily by an imposing apartment building above the intersection of NW 23rd Avenue and Burnside Street. Perhaps that's why, after spending most of my working life on the East Coast, when I retired to Portland fifty years later and found the Envoy Apartments still standing, I decided to live there. A fellow tenant told me that John Reed, whom I admired as Portland's most famous Red, was born just above our building.[1] The steps at our back door that led up to SW Cactus Drive, he said, were all that remained of Reed's grandfather's mansion.

The City of Portland named the next street over in honor of Reed's grandfather—Henry Dodge Green—who one biographer says "got rich by swindling Indian tribes out of precious furs and using the profits to build water, gas, and iron empires."[2] But evidently embarrassed by the radical offspring of such an exploiter, Portland officially ignored his grandson until a century after his birth. That made a perverse sort of sense to me: after all, don't those with the power to bestow municipal honors ensure they reflect dominant values rather than dissident ones?

Still, I considered the excitement stirred in me by sharing the physical space that had been occupied by John Reed to be similar to that evoked in visitors to more conventional historic sites. Could sites associated with such controversial Portlanders as Reed contribute to public interest in an alternative local history? Were those steps from SW Cactus Drive the first site to tell a story? Such musings inspired this *Portland Red Guide* and continue to guide this second edition.

I am grateful to that neighbor and the many friends, acquaintances, and informants who guided me to what is collected here. First were a quartet of visitors to my Gearhart beach shack—Steve Vause, Carlyn

Synaven, Brooke Jacobson, and the late Susan Wheeler—to whom I evidently could not suppress my enthusiasm for exploring stories and sites of local radical history. Perhaps in an effort to quiet me down, they suggested, "Why don't you write it down?"

Many of the other people whom I pestered for information are already gone: Hank and Martina Gangle Curl, Elmer Buehler, Jesse Stranahan, Doug Lynch, Marvin Ricks, Eugene Snyder, Eileen Cooke and Gene Klare; Old Men's Club members Ken Fitzgerald, Nick Chaivoe, Jim Canon, Sam Markson, Virginia Malbin, and Ben Brostoff; and Oregon Cultural Heritage Commission colleagues Fred DeWolfe, Robb Tuttle, Jim Kopp, and Marion Wood Kolisch. But some I can again credit in this second edition are surviving: Old Men's Club members Charlie Grossman, Ed and Alice Beechert, and Howard Glazer, and OCHC colleagues as Tim Barnes, David Horowitz, Phil Wikelund, Dory Hylton, Janet Kreft, David Hedges, Walt Curtis, and David Milholland, who urged me to stay with the project when my energy faltered. Also Ken Dragoon, Norm Diamond, Harry Stein, Peter Sleeth, Lois Stranahan, and many more whom I can only blame a diminished short-term memory for failing to acknowledge.

Ironically, one of the most rewarding sources for this guide was the archive of the Portland Police Bureau's infamous Red Squad, which contains records of its hostile spying on radicals, labor organizers, and civil rights and peace activists from the 1920s to the 1980s. It includes the Red Squad files illegally taken home by the late police officer Winfield Falk, a right wing ideologue exposed by *The Portland Tribune* in 2002. It was Marcus Robbins, former city archivist, and assistant archivist Brian Johnson, who introduced me to, and guided me through, that precious but outrageous material. Also, the staff of the Oregon Historical Society's research library have been special friends during the many years I have spent asking for their help. I became familiar with its collection of newspaper files, city directories and above all for a guide to historic sites, its copy of the street renaming index.

Extra credit should be granted to the skilled, dedicated, and enthusiastic students in Portland State University's book publishing program, under direction from Dennis Stovall, and his faculty. The first edition took shape under the care of Terra Chapek, Abbey Gaterud, Gloria Harrison, Vinnie Kinsella, and Carson Smith, while this second was guided by Anna Noak and Amanda Gomm.

Special homage is due Kim MacColl, dean of local historians, whose monumental three-volume history of Portland pierced the fawning aura which conventional treatments had placed on its political and business leaders.[3] The late Gordon DeMarco, who distilled much of MacColl and added some original research,[4] was another valuable source. I should not forget Kim Fern's charming radical bike tour,[5] or Icky A's uniquely observed, informal radical history.[6] Elsewhere, I was impressed by Bruce Kayton's *Radical Walking Tours of New York City* (2003), for which Pete Seeger wrote the introduction. And finally, my thanks to the many informants too numerous to be listed who confirmed, added, and corrected my original efforts. This new edition benefits greatly from their help.

They all deserve whatever credit may come the *Red Guide*'s way, but no responsibility whatsoever for my own remaining errors, omissions, or poor judgments.

—Michael Munk

PREFACE NOTES

1. Gary Dennis, proprietor of a video store for film enthusiasts, had a similar epiphany when he read that his street, W. 103rd in Manhattan, was Humphrey Bogart's childhood home.

2. Tamara Hovey, *John Reed: Witness to Revolution* (New York: Crown Pub, 1975). Even the more polite biographers say Green's wealth was "derived from a particularly noxious form of commerce." Richard O'Connor and Dale L. Walker, *The Lost Revolutionary: A Biography of John Reed* (New York: Harcourt Brace, 1967).

3. E. Kimbark MacColl, *The Shaping of a City* (Portland, OR: Georgian Press, 1976); MacColl, *The Growth of a City* (Portland, OR: Georgian Press, 1979); MacColl and Harry H. Stein, *Merchants, Money, and Power* (Portland, OR: Georgian Press, 1988).

4. Gordon DeMarco, *A Short History of Portland* (San Francisco: Lexikos, 1990).

5. Kim Fern, "Portland Radical History Bike Tour" from Lewis and Clark College Political Economy Program (2002), http://www.lclark.edu/~polyecon/history%20tour.htm. See also: Jason Wilson et al., "Jason's Portland Radical History-Tour" from Platial: the People's Atlas, http://www.platial.com/jason/map/5163.

6. "Livin' in Doom Town: History, Albina Gentrification, Dr. Marie Equi & Other Resistance," *Nosedive* 8 1997.

HOW TO USE

THE PORTLAND RED GUIDE

This rally, on August 1, 1932, was held outside the Japanese Consulate in downtown Portland. Protesters called for withdrawal from foreign wars, payment of the bonus, and other radical causes. *City of Portland Archives, A2001-074.92.*

By linking our radical history to physical sites, I hope to bring back to life and recognition the radical and dissenting history of Portlanders—even if the physical evidence of their life and times no longer exists. May such modest sites evoke reflection on Portland's radicals and their choices. May they at least challenge readers as Francis X. Clines did, in expressing hope for a book on the consequences of a rumored slave revolt in eighteenth century New York: such a book would "burden any modern attempt at strolling the city's streets in a spirit of innocence."[1]

It will soon become apparent to users of this guide that the sites listed are rarely physically impressive or emotionally evocative. Architecturally significant sites, such as the Pittock Mansion, are most often monuments to the privileges of the winners rather than the ordinarily impoverished losers. So if we come upon, for example, the unremarkable house on SW Hall Street that was home to radicals Dr. Marie Equi and Elizabeth Gurley Flynn, it's rather the link to their roles in local and international radical history that might stir our curiosity, not the structure itself. Similarly, the downtown site of the Portland Police Bureau's Red Squad in the 1930s is listed in the guide to reveal its infamous and continuing role in suppression and harassment of local radicals. However, there is nothing threatening or exceptional in what was then the Railway Exchange Building, and today is called the Oregon Pioneer Building. As the director of the Bosco-Milligan Foundation, Cathy Galbraith noted in its register of Portland's black community's historic buildings, "Sometimes a historic building doesn't look the way we think a historic building should," but it should be respected because its "walls have witnessed history being made."[2]

Finally, during the writing of the *Red Guide* and this second edition, several sites yielded to the creed of "highest and best use" and were destroyed to enhance the profits of real estate speculators. Rather than eliminating the historic link entirely, the *Red Guide* notes at least some of those former sites. Readers seeking natural or man-made splendor, of which Portland boasts a fair share, are referred to page 221, Recommended Portland Histories, at the end. The guide groups sites in Portland and its vicinity into six broad historical periods which reflect how different radical and militant movements responded to the historical challenges of the day. Each period is introduced with a brief but pointed summary of its major trends and developments. The sites associated with each historical period are then generally arranged chronologically and numbered consecutively through the entire guide. The periods are:

> The Nineteenth Century (Utopians & Marxists)
> 1900–1930 (Wobblies & Socialists)
> 1930s (Unions & Commies)
> WWII–1960 (McCarthyism & Cold War)
> 1960–1973 (Peaceniks & Civil Rights)
> 1974–Present (Identities & Protests)

The significance of each listing in Portland's human history is briefly assessed and is often illustrated. Listings are numbered sequentially with a square icon and the entry's title, like this:

7 FIREBRAND

Maps are found at the end of each section. To find locations discussed in the text, look for the square icon on the maps. Throughout the book, if the subject of an entry is referred to elsewhere in the guide, the text, with the appropriate section and listing number, will be highlighted in red (e.g. **Louise Bryant** 30 in John Reed's listing). Within listings, titles are highlighted (e.g. **Ruth Barnett**), as are addresses (e.g. *4056 N. Williams Avenue*).

In each historical period, first mentions of organizations use the names in full with an abbreviation, but subsequent references within that period use just the abbreviations. For example, the first reference to the Industrial Workers of the World in section A is followed by the abbreviation (IWW), and subsequent references within that section are just the IWW. If a quick reference is needed, a list of frequently used acronyms is included on page 222.

The reader can use the guide in several ways. Reading the section introductions consecutively offers an informal narrative of Portland's radical history. Using the map and its location keys serves as a street or neighborhood guide to nearby sites. And for readers whose curiosity is aroused by a person, event, or organization on these pages—as is strongly hoped—consulting the endnotes, references, and suggested books and websites may be a first step toward becoming intimately familiar with their chosen subjects.

HOW TO USE THE PORTLAND RED GUIDE NOTES

1. "New York Burning: Gotham Witch Hunt," *New York Times*, October 2, 2005. In 1741, following false rumors of a slave revolt, thirty slaves and four whites were burned at the stake.

2. Darrell Millner, et al., *Cornerstones of the Community: Buildings of Portland's African American History* (Portland, OR: The Bosco-Milligan Foundation, 1995).

INTRODUCTION

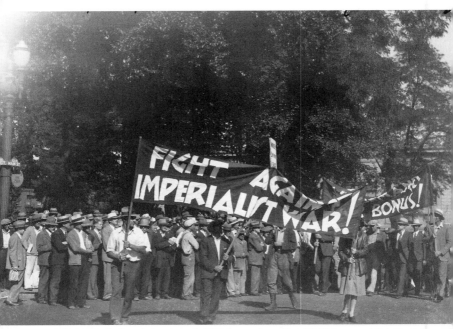

Radicals in Portland marched on August 1, 1932, in an antiwar rally at SW 4th Avenue and Main Street. As the marchers passed, a huge crowd looked on. *City of Portland Archives, A2001-074.90.*

CLASS WAR AND REVOLUTION IN PORTLAND?

Portland's business and political leaders sure thought so. On the morning of June 8, 1934, the Board of Directors of the Portland Chamber of Commerce called an emergency session to hear a report from a select committee of several of their most prominent members. West Coast longshoremen had been on strike for a month, demanding union recognition and a shorter workweek. The city's business leaders declared the strike a "siege on Portland industry."[1] Citing closed mills, rotting perishables on the docks, and industries shut down from lack of supplies, they denounced the city's police as insufficiently enthusiastic about protecting strikebreakers and the state's governor as unwilling to call out the National Guard. When they demanded decisive action to break the strike, the business leaders were warned by an Army intelligence officer, "Portland is the worst hot spot in which to release troops at this time because if there is a revolution in the making, such action would precipitate it." Although fully aware that "it would doubtless lead to bloodshed and perhaps loss of life," the business leaders charged its select committee to consider hiring armed vigilantes ("deputized volunteers," it called them) to do the job.

The action group was chaired by Horace Mecklem, manager of the Oregon office of the New England Mutual Life Insurance Company, and included four other leading citizens: Henry Cabell of the Failing Estate, retired U.S. Army General Creed Hammond, attorney Ralph Hamilton, and lumberman Aubrey Watzek. Under the manifesto, "We must end this strike by peaceful means if possible, but if necessary, by other means," they urged the Chamber to raise a private army to break the strike. The Chamber's members, in turn, with full appreciation that their vigilante army would probably cause bloodshed, signed on without recorded dissent. They set up a front organization called the Citizens Emergency Committee, which the Oregon State Federation of Labor named the "silk stocking mob," and authorized it to hire between one thousand and five thousand vigilantes, whom the Chamber demanded Mayor Joseph Carson deputize as special police. With its private army of deputized police, the Chamber hoped to suppress Portland's "revolution in the making."

Governor Julius L. Meier (of the Meier & Frank department store) also saw the potential of revolutionary violence. Pleading with President Franklin Roosevelt to send federal troops, Meier declared, "We are now in a state of armed hostilities." He warned of an "insurrection, which, if not checked, could lead to civil war." After the President refused, Meier briefly mobilized Oregon National Guard troops at the Armory on NW 11th Avenue (now the home of Portland Center Stage's theater) before sending them to wait at a camp outside Portland.

The vigilantes hired by the "silk stocking mob" brought out the poet in some of the striking longshoremen, who published their efforts in the strike bulletin, *The Hook*. One read:

> They must feel proud to be neatly clad
> In those "he-man" suits of olive drab;
> With a real live gun and a "billy" too,
> They plan great deeds, 'ere they are through.
> But our real men oft' have to smile,
> As they watch the specials all the while;
> Whole faces they have, though it won't be long
> Till they'll wonder just where their nose has gone.
> — P. F. Freeman

The mellow Portland of contemporary reputation and conventional history stands in sharp contrast to this remarkable episode from its past. Although conservative media such as *The Oregonian* may complain that the city's political culture consists only of the "kinda-liberal, liberal and commie pinko,"[2] most actual Lefties would respond, "Don't we wish." In any case, our opening story of Portland's brush with revolution more than seventy years ago confirms that its past includes some dramatic episodes largely ignored in our public history.

The main purpose of the *Red Guide* is to offer a respectful rendering of the mostly forgotten people, organizations, and events that challenged the dominant powers of their day in the name of justice and equality—of which the victory of the 1934 strikers is a remarkable exception to a long list of defeats. An informal guide to Portland's radical past, the *Red Guide* links notable radicals, their organizations, and their activities to physical sites associated with them. It honors those that the mainstream histories of Portland largely ignore.[3]

WHO GETS TO NAME?

> *Some of them have left behind a name so others can declare their praise. Of others, there is no memory; they have perished as though they never existed. But these were also godly men, whose righteous deeds have not been forgotten.*[4]

Like any other town, Portland sketches a public version of its history to residents and visitors through the names it chooses to bestow on city streets, buildings, parks, and natural features. The criteria for its more elevated celebrations (memorial plaques, commemorative monuments, published histories, and guides) are more selective. Few will be surprised that the honored names and sites are overwhelmingly those of Portland's land speculators and big businessmen, the winners in what has frequently been a corrupt struggle for profits from land and resource exploitation, and those fallen in American military missions—whether worthy or not.[5] As current Mayor Sam Adams observed during the 2006 vote to rename North Portland Boulevard as Rosa Parks Way, "Most of Portland's streets are named for dead white developers or their daughters."

Alon Raab added it up: "Portland streets bear the names of 100 businessmen, 92 landowners, 69 public officials, 46 real estate [speculators], 39 churchmen, 23 military men, and 7 lawyers."[6] Raab then exercised his imagination to make his point:

> *Riding my bike down John Reed Avenue, I turned towards tree-lined Louise Bryant Way and continued past Mark Rothko Plaza to War Resisters Square. It was a good feeling to move along paths bearing the names of two early twentieth century writers and revolutionaries and a painter with strong ties to our city, and wind up at a place commemorating peace. But the sharp horn*

> *of a restless driver awoke me from my reveries...I was hurled*
> *back to a city [whose names] hail not the people and deeds*
> *that contributed to my life, but captains of industry, politicians*
> *and corporations...As I ride along streets celebrating conquest*
> *and greed, I yearn for a time when such Portlanders as Linus*
> *Pauling and Don Chambers would be acknowledged. I keep*
> *hoping and pedaling.*

Urban critic Lewis Mumford succinctly nailed the natural history of the American city from the beginning of the nineteenth century to the present day when he described it as "a private commercial venture to be carved up in any fashion that might increase the turnover and further the rise in land values."[7] At a 1938 address to the **City Club of Portland** 167, Mumford was impolite enough to denounce "certain persons" in his audience who were "licking their chops and counting their gold" from land speculation along the Columbia River and profit from Bonneville Dam. Why the French-born Benjamin Bonneville (1796–1878) was honored with that pioneering project is questionable. He was a commercial explorer for John Jacob Astor whose efforts to establish relations with Native Americans were disastrous, and he was eventually court-martialed by the U.S. Army for "misbehaving before the enemy" in the Mexican–American war.

If the official take on Portland's history celebrates only the values of a narrow part of the city's past, it can only tell a biased story. That bias not only relegates dissidents to "the dust bin of history," but also glosses over the corruption, stolen wealth, and crimes that enabled the winners. As the late Portland journalist Dean Collins asked, "Where do the leading businessmen, entrepreneurs, and real estate developers— many whose names appear on street signs and monuments—fit into the generation of dirty politics?" His answer: "Everywhere...Portland only pretended it was different."[8]

The following *Oregonian* excerpt about the methods used to register "frequenters of dives" north of W. Burnside illustrates the political corruption that plagued Portland's past:

> *Some 10 days ago a well-known heeler went out on the streets*
> *and gathered in frequenters of dives, whom he led to the*

*Eagle saloon, on First and Burnside streets, telling them that
by coming there they would confer a favor on Police Sergeant
Church. Once there, their names and ages were taken, and each
was assigned a room in some North End lodging house. After
the heeler had thrown a couple of $20 gold pieces on the bar
and bought several rounds of drinks for all hands, they were
loaded in three shipments on the First-Street car, taken thence
to Washington, thence to Fifth and to the Courthouse, where
they were duly registered by the heeler. That sort of thing has
been going on in the North End for weeks, and such people may
be depended upon to come out and vote the Simon ticket at the
primaries tomorrow.*

*Arrangements having been made for a full vote of the hobos and
North End dive frequenters, it is urged that businessmen offset it
by allowing their employees every opportunity to go to the polls
tomorrow.*
— *The Oregonian*, February 23, 1902

*Tell me how you call a place, and I will tell who you are and
what is important to you.*
—Alon Raab, 1999

The significance of the power to name streets, cities, and even
nations becomes clearest in the wake of revolution. When capitalism
was restored in formerly socialist countries, nations such as the Soviet
Union, Yugoslavia, and Czechoslovakia broke apart and were renamed.
The pre-revolutionary names of St. Petersburg and Chemnitz replaced
Leningrad and Karl-Marx-Stadt. But that political sea change could
not dislodge the name of **Paul Robeson 136**, a frequent but controversial
visitor to Portland, from the Berlin street named in his honor.

Portlanders witnessed the political significance of street names during World War I, when most streets with Germanic references were
renamed, as if to clarify who our nation's enemy was. In the Brooklyn
neighborhood, Frankfurt Street became our French ally Lafayette,

and nearby Bismarck became Bush. Liebe Street, however, was spared because the City Council declared its pioneer namesake to have been a "loyal American."

Portland has some rules for naming its infrastructure, but in its rush to rename the most prominent portion of historic Front Avenue in honor of the late civic entrepreneur and World War II deportee Bill Naito, it violated a rule requiring the subject of a nomination to have been dead for five years. On the other hand, proposals to rename the Fremont Bridge over the Willamette River for the late Oregon Senator Wayne Morse have not succeeded, suggesting the outspoken opponent of the Vietnam War remains too controversial. What's wrong with Fremont? **Julia Ruuttila's** 175 poem "The Fremont Bridge" explains:

> It dominates the skyline in Northwest,
> A high-arched span dwarfing the station clocks,
> Montgomery [Park], St. Helen's icy rocks.
> Named for a man who never knew or guessed
> The changes that time would bring to the west.
> Pathfinder, soldier, pioneer—
> Not with the plow—the sextant and sword
> Were his true symbols, and that time is past... [9]

There are important lessons to be learned from the lengthy struggle—with racist undertones—to rename Union Avenue (originally celebrating the North's victory in the Civil War) as Martin Luther King Jr. Boulevard. In the 1980s, the original proposal to honor King by renaming downtown's Front Avenue for the civil rights martyr was blocked by the vigorous opposition of Portland's business leaders. The Portland City Council then voted to shift the name to Union Avenue in 1989, but a racist petition demanding the City Council's decision be put to a public vote was circulated by the late fundamentalist Christian and former Republican state chair Walter Huss. Remarkably, fifty-one thousand Portlanders supported it. It was not until 1995 that the name was finally legitimated[10] when the Oregon Supreme Court ruled that naming streets was not subject to citizen initiatives because it was an administrative act, not a legislative one. Even then, persistent opponents, still led by Huss, tried but failed to change MLK Boulevard back to Union Avenue.

Don't dig up the past! Dwell on the past and you'll lose an eye.
Forget the past and you'll lose both eyes.
—Old Russian proverb

Resistance to memorials of people of color is a persistent scenario in Portland politics. A statue in King's honor was erected in front of the Oregon Convention Center at *777 NE* MLK *Boulevard* several years later. More recently, the impact of the civil rights movement on racism permitted naming a school for the black freedom fighter Harriet Tubman; and in 2006 the new Rosa Parks School, named for the late anti-segregation heroine, was opened in the former World War II public housing complex, the rebuilt New Columbia Homes. The same year, proposals to rename Portland Boulevard "Rosa Parks Way" overcame opposition when the city council voted to make the change. In 2009, resistance persisted against renaming SE 39th Avenue for Cesar Chavez.

It was Oregon, all right: the place where stories begin that end
someplace else...There are worse things.
—H.L. Davis, 1953

Today, names that evoke the original inhabitants of the land that became Portland survive mainly in the names of counties, while some references to Indian places by white settlers, such as the many Oregon creeks and other geographical features named for "Squaws," were decreed politically incorrect by the state legislature in 2001. In the early nineteenth century, the Portland/Vancouver basin was home to a resident population of four to five thousand Chinookian people that would swell to nearly ten thousand during the spring salmon run—one of the densest populations of American Indians north of Mexico.[11] Historically, the Chinook tribe of the Multnomah lived along the Columbia from Sauvie Island to the Sandy River, while the Clackamas, Tualatin, and Clowewalla favored the area around the falls of the Willamette River at Oregon City. When President Thomas Jefferson sent his 1803 military expedition here "for the purposes of commerce," his Corps of Discovery passed Neerchokikoo, a village where Portland International Airport now stands. The village contained twenty-five houses, fifty canoes, and two hundred residents called "Flatheads" by Lewis and Clark.

John McLoughlin, the British Hudson Bay Company's fur impresario, has a highway named for him between Portland and Oregon City. In contrast, the names of the five members of the Cayuse tribe who resisted Christian efforts to convert them—Telakite, Tomahas, Clokomas, Isiaasheluckas, and Kiamasumkin—are not found on Oregon City's Main Street. That's where Joe Meek, another celebrated pioneer hero for whom a Portland school is named, hanged them in sight of McLoughlin's mansion before more than one thousand spectators. Some historians and tribal members consider the 1850 execution that followed a trial run by Judge Orville "Slippery as a Greased Eel" Pratt to be "nothing more than a public lynching."[12]

From 1843, when the first provisional government formed a militia, until the United States invaded Cuba and the Philippines in 1898, Oregon soldiers fought only the native resistance—the Cayuse, Modoc, Nez Perce, and Bannock-Paiutes—killing almost two thousand of them while suffering less than one hundred dead. During the Civil War, many Oregonians expressed support for the South. In 1860, Oregon U.S. Senator Joseph Lane was the vice-presidential candidate on the pro-slavery, or "Copperhead," Democratic ticket. A majority of the state's Democratic papers backed Lane, including *The Oregon Democrat* (Albany), *The Union* (Corvallis), *Jacksonville Sentinel*, *Eugene Herald*, *Roseburg Express*, and *Portland Daily News*. Five pro-Confederacy newspapers were banned from the mails, including the *Oregon Democrat*, the *Union*, the *Jacksonville Southern Oregon Gazette*, and the daily *Portland Advertiser*.

As the Portland Traction Company saw fit to illustrate on one of its weekly passes in 1937, most of Oregon's one thousand eight hundred Union soldiers did not engage the Confederacy but "pursued Native Americans around the Northwest."[13]

Major Melville Wilkinson led some of those "Indian fighters" in Oregon after the Civil War. He was killed in action in 1896 during what some consider the last armed resistance of Native Americans when a band of Chippewas stood up at the Battle of Sugar Point (now Minnesota).

By the middle of the nineteenth century, Indian lands had been commercially or forcibly transformed through the Doctrine of Discovery[14] into a raw commercial venture called Portland (for its namesakes in Maine and England) and carved up among a handful of land speculators.

The most prominent of these speculators were Asa Lovejoy, Francis Pettygrove, William Chapman, Daniel H. Lownsdale, and Stephen Coffin. They were soon followed by sea and riverboat captains Ankeny, Couch, Flanders, Hoyt, Irving, and Marshall. Among them, only Coffin's unfortunate name is absent today from any Portland street, school, or park.

By the end of the century, Portland had followed the natural pattern of urban development as power shifted from ownership of land to industry, utility franchises, railroads, banking, and trade. Winners in those enterprises—the Corbetts, Ladds, and Ainsworths, together with the MacLeays, Burnsides, Starks, and Bybees—joined the earlier speculators to become familiar names on the growing city's municipal landmarks. While wealth was a prerequisite to put a name on an official map, it was insufficient if not accumulated by Christian Anglo-Saxons. The official seal of the city includes the Star of David, but the city's wealthy Jewish families, the Hirsches, Franks, Goldsmiths, Sellings, and Meiers had to build or buy the properties that carry their names.

Women, even those associated with powerful men and not known as dissenters, are almost absent from Portland place names. Local historian Eugene Snyder finds only North Ida Avenue and North Minerva Avenue in the St. Johns neighborhood and SW Bertha—all the first names of wives of nineteenth-century land speculators.[15] Duniway School may have been named for Abigail the suffragist, but her given name isn't on it.

Finally, readers might be curious to know whom NE Marx Street commemorates, especially since the union halls of Bricklayers Local 1 and Cement Masons Local 555 are located at 12812 NE Marx Street. Given the bias in bestowing municipal names, it's safe to assume that it wasn't for Karl. On the other hand, between 1904 and 1907, Karl Marx was the name of a post office on the Oregon coast. Today, it's known as Neskowin. And, **Karl Marx Saltveit 55** proudly identified an east Portland barbershop with his anglicized name (Carl Marx) in the 1930s.

Only a few of Portland's radicals, their organizations, or related events are officially acknowledged. The PGE Park TriMet stop offers a maintenance building decorated with writer Robert Sullivan's references to **Dr. Marie Equi 16**, **John Reed 31**, *Firebrand* 7, and **Beatrice Morrow Cannady 34**, the first black woman to graduate from the Northwest School of Law in 1922, as well as a copy of a handbill defending labor leader Harry Bridges. TriMet's Portland Expo Center stop honors deported **Japanese**

American Oregonians 96 moved from the location's former livestock exposition center to concentration camps during World War II. There is a park bench and plaque erected by the private Oregon Cultural Heritage Commission honoring John Reed near his birthplace in Washington Park, as well as two local private memorials in Wallace Park, and another at Reed College to commemorate **Benjamin Linder** 177, murdered by President Reagan's Contras in Nicaragua. Perhaps most imposing is the remarkable and little known homage paid by the federal—not the city—government to **Woody Guthrie** 91, at the Bonneville Power Administration's headquarters. Since 1990, Portland radicals, led by members of the band General Strike, have commemorated **Joe Hill** 19 on November 19, the date of the Wobbly organizer and songmaster's murder by the state of Utah. The single exception to the city's (and Oregon's) reluctance to honor local labor leaders may have been the floating dock on the Willamette River in downtown Portland that was named for longshore leader **Francis Murnane** 171. But the city destroyed it in 2009 in an act of "city-sponsored vandalism."

Of course, there is no massive, popular demand in Portland that radicals or their works should be commemorated. Many Portlanders probably agree with the Kent, Ohio resident who dissented from a proposal for a memorial to the four students killed by National Guard troops while protesting during the Vietnam War, observing, "If for every death in a social movement anywhere in the U.S. we put up a memorial, we'd have them all over the place." But another Kent resident confirmed that ideology remains the dominant force in deciding who gets to be honored. Those who were killed in the 1970 "Kent State Massacre," he said, were only "some hippie college students who didn't know the meaning of law and order," and expressed a typical know-nothing view of history itself. "We should have stopped talking about them a long, long time ago."[16]

FINAL THOUGHTS

> The endeavor
> To interpret a city
> Airily,
> By a mere wave of one's words —
> Presumptuous
> A task for fools.
> Come, fool!
> — Mary Carolyn Davies, 1924

From the nineteenth century, when the earliest sites in this guide are dated, to the present day, many Portlanders have challenged the conventional wisdom that a capitalist economic system provides the best opportunities for personal and economic freedom and prosperity. As enshrined in stained glass over a hundred years ago in British Columbia's provincial capital building, the dominant credo has been: "The [capitalist] economy: without it, no wealth; with it, no poverty." But local radicals used to argue much more vigorously than today that prosperity for the few depended on the suffering of a large reserve labor force of poor, unorganized workers and small family farmers. They exposed the hypocrisy of capitalists who argued that accepting the risks of a free market exempted them from any public oversight while, as owners of railroads and lumber and mining companies, they used their political muscle to exploit public land and its natural resources. The early populists and environmentalists, who argued that such public treasure should be reserved for the benefit of the people, lost a righteous, but hardly equal, struggle.

Those who believe that the public has access to a "free market of ideas" must confront the historic fact—for which this guide provides the example of Portland in 1934—that whenever those with vested private economic interests imagined any serious challenge to their dominance, they could count on obliging city and state authorities to suppress the threat. The most ferocious government persecutions of such radicals were conducted during the first Red Scare following World War I and the Russian Revolution, and again in the McCarthy Era following the Soviet-United States victory in World War II.

Only a few of their names can be found in our schoolbooks. Fewer still stand in marble or bronze in our halls and parks. The mass of Americans knows little or nothing about them. Never mind. They dreamed nobly, and they acted.
—Stewart Holbrook, 1957

It remains the dominant contemporary American ideology that something called human nature demonstrates that capitalism provides the most natural model for organizing our economic, social, political, and cultural affairs. Acting on the belief that all are born selfish and programmed to compete against everyone else may indeed help one survive in our present system and occasionally even succeed. But capitalism motivates people not only by offering the carrot of opportunity to an aspiring Nike entrepreneur, but also the stick of what awaits losers, publicly displayed on skidroad—as Portland's lower W. Burnside Street was known.

Most of the people, organizations, and events commemorated in this guide challenge that view of human nature. They testify, to the contrary, that many of them were motivated to improve the condition of the world rather than their personal status in it. Its historical listings call attention to those who insisted on a better justification for their lives than "success" in the struggle for material wealth, and so dedicated themselves to offering alternative visions of how to organize our economic and social affairs. That so far the majority of us have not been persuaded to sign on to their proposals, or that some of them gave up or even eventually succumbed to the dominant ideology, does not diminish the worth of their struggle.

Unfortunately, too often our standards for evaluating social movements pivot around whether or not they "succeeded" in realizing their visions rather than on the merits or powers of the visions themselves. By such a measure, virtually every radical movement failed because the basic power relations they sought to change remain pretty much intact. And yet it is precisely these alternative visions and dreams that inspire new generations to continue to struggle for change.
—Robin D.G. Kelley, Freedom Dreams

Mike Davis succinctly expressed a bias, similar to that which readers will no doubt discover in this guide, when he stated, "The finest embodiments of moral courage in American history [were the] Abolitionists, the **Wobblies 17**, the **Abraham Lincoln Brigade 78**, and the Student Nonviolent Coordinating Committee." [17] But a listing in this book does not attest that a person has an unblemished political and personal history, nor that all the activities of every organization or every radical event were justified or successful. Adopting such standards would produce a small volume indeed, and if municipal officials used them, they would find it difficult to name any of our parks and streets. It should also become evident that not every one of our listees may have looked back on their radical activities with pride; indeed a few may have done so with great regret. No matter. The impulse they shared—the struggle for a better world rather than for their individual prospects in the existing one—is a righteous commitment that deserves wider and more generous public recognition.

INTRODUCTION NOTES

1. Michael Munk, "Portland's 'Silk Stocking Mob': The Citizens Emergency League in the 1934 Maritime Strike," *Pacific Northwest Quarterly*, Summer 2000:150–60. Reprinted in John Trombold and Peter Donahue (eds), *Reading Portland: The City in Prose* (Portland, OR: Historical Society Press, 2006). All quotes related to these 1934 events are from the files of the Portland Chamber of Commerce, held in the University of Oregon Library's special collections. They are fully documented in the above-noted article.

2. Ryan Frank, "A clear case of the blues," *The Oregonian*, July 6, 2006.

3. The distortion or selective ignoring of dissident history is not confined to Portland. See James W. Loewen, *Lies My Teacher Told Me: Everything Your American History Textbook Got Wrong* (New York: New Press, 1995).

4. This biblical quote was used by the granddaughter of CIA director William Colby at his funeral. It begins by acknowledging rulers known for their valor and advisors for their intelligence but honors CIA agents killed in the line of duty for whom there is "no memory."

5. Dolores Hayden, *The Power of Place: Urban Landscapes as Public History* (Cambridge, MA: MIT Press, 1995) observes that the many equestrian statues of white males and cannons in the municipal parks of American cities are inspired by "John Wayne conquest stories." In 2006, critics opposed a Salem statue commemorating the U.S. soldiers who died in the Iraq invasion and occupation as premature and supportive of an unpopular war.

6. Alon Raab, "Place names are about who has power," *The Portland Alliance*, May 1999.

7. Lewis Mumford, *The City in History* (New York: Harcourt, Brace & World, 1961) 426.

8. Quoted by John Terry, "Dirty Deeds Shaped Early Portland, too," *Oregon's Trails*, *The Oregonian*, November 20, 2005.

9. Julia Ruuttila, *This is My Shadow* (Self-published manuscript, 1989).

10. John Terry, "Ladd's House Stands its Ground," *Oregon's Trails, The Oregonian*, April 16, 2006. The U.S. Geological Survey, with advice from state authorities such as the Oregon Geographic Names Board, decides the names of natural things: rivers, mountains, some historic sites. But roads, parks, etc. are "administrative designations...bestowed by the government under whose jurisdiction they fall—states, counties, cities, park districts, etc."

11. Robert T. Boyd and Yvonne P. Hayda, "Seasonal Population Movement along the Lower Columbia River: the Social and Ecological Context," *American Ethnologist* (1987) 309–25.

12. "Cold Trail of Pioneer Mystery Reaches Present," The Oregonian, September 29, 1996. Also see Ronald Lansing, *The Juggernaut: The Whitman Massacre Trial of 1850* (Pasadena, CA: Ninth Judicial Circuit Historical Society, 1993).

13. Frances Fuller Victor, *The Early Indian Wars of Oregon* (Salem, OR: F. C. Baker, state printer, 1894).

14. The Doctrine of Discovery legitimized "Christian" hegemony over Indian ("infidels, heathens, and savages") lands and was confirmed by the Supreme Court (*Johnson v. McIntosh*) in 1823. See also *Oregon's Future: a nonpartisan public affairs magazine*, Winter 2006, 68.

15. Eugene Snyder, *Portland Names and Neighborhoods* (Portland, OR: Binford and Mort Publishing, 1979).

16. *The Oregonian*, July 16, 1998.

17. Mike Davis, a former Reed student, is a "Marxist environmentalist" who teaches at the University of California, Irvine. Perhaps his best known work is *City of Quartz: Excavating the Future in Los Angeles* (London: Verso, 1990).

CHAPTER ONE

UTOPIANS & MARXISTS

1804–1899

This unidentified man used his donkey and cart to protest the actions of the powerful. His signs read "Free All Class Prisoners," "We're Against the Raw Deal & Stacked Deck," and "No Race Hatred." *City of Portland Archives, A2001-074.36.*

*Until the lions have their historians, tales of hunting will always
glorify the hunter.*
—African proverb

T he early history of dissenting Portland is largely the story of
people responding to the nation's uneven economic past and
expansionist adventures abroad. The earliest listings include
local manifestations of late nineteenth-century populist agrarian, working class, and anti-imperialist movements—a time that historian E.
Kimbark MacColl characterizes as one of "private enterprise at the
public trough." Against the devotion to laissez-faire capitalism that
was the dominant ideology of the time, some early organizations of
wage workers were inspired by Karl Marx's systematic critique of that
economic system. The earliest such organization was the **Socialist Labor
Party (SLP)** 2. Its Marxist ideology dates from 1890, but the party traces
itself to the Workingmen's Party in 1876. A Portland branch of the SLP
continues to this day, educating its mainly elderly members in a strict
version of working-class Marxism that remains critical of rival socialist
organizations. They meet monthly at the Central Library.[1]

Firebrand 7, a national anarchist newspaper, was published 1895–1897
from a farm in Sellwood until the federal government suppressed it for
obscenity. A sense of how conservative Portlanders regarded anarchists
can be gleaned from a December 1901 article in *The Oregonian*:

> An anarchist of the genuine stripe visited all that district south of
> Powell Street Saturday, peddling from house to house literature,
> whose teaching was the long line of anarchism. He carried with
> him several publications which he offered for sale at all the
> houses visited. He timed his visits when he felt sure he would
> only find the women at home, about 4 o'clock in the afternoon.

> To those who declined to purchase papers of him, and very few
> did buy from him, he was very insulting. He said, among other
> things, that, "Roosevelt would go the same way McKinley did,
> and it will not be long. It would serve him right, too."

Less exclusive and sectarian than the anarchists or the Marxist SLP was an agrarian and working-class populist movement that blamed plutocratic monopolies and bankers for the recurring depressions that regularly cost millions of people their farms and jobs. The populists also opposed imperialistic adventures like the Spanish-American War, which, they charged, sent poor people to war to enhance the profits of the rich. Male Oregonians (women could not vote until 1913) expressed support for that movement through the
. In 1892, the Populist Party's presidential candidate, James Weaver, won 34 percent of the state's male population's ballots and sent several of its members to the state legislature. Four years later, 48 percent of Oregon voters backed William Jennings Bryan's coalition of the Populist Party, Democrats, and a splinter of Republicans. Bryan fell only two thousand votes behind the winner William McKinley, whose victory MacColl credits to "massive vote fraud."

In 1887, Oregon was the first state to formally declare the first Monday in September as Labor Day. Although it was later used to discourage American workers from observing the more radical international May Day, the Grand Marshal of New York's first Labor Day parade declared that the day was intended to "offer monopolists and their tools in both political parties such a sight as will make them think more profoundly." In recent years, Portlanders have observed both May Day and Labor Day.

Members of Portland's working class joined **Coxey's Army 6** in 1893 in its march on Washington to demand jobs for the unemployed.

Portland's municipal government and its business leaders celebrated what the radicals and populists opposed, and they heaped special honor on the first major military effort of U.S. imperialism. The Second Oregon Volunteer Infantry Regiment's (today's National Guard) participation in the 1898 invasion and occupation of the Philippines is celebrated in **Lownsdale Square 9**. Together with today's Chapman Square, the adjoining squares are called the Plaza Blocks. In 1922, Portland also honored a hero of the 1898 U.S. invasion of Cuba—a greater success than its more recent effort at the Bay of Pigs—with A.

Phimister Proctor's mounting of Rough Rider Teddy Roosevelt, on his horse, in the Park Blocks before the Portland Art Museum. Relics of the battleship *Oregon*, which participated both in the Philippine and Cuban invasions and the U.S. intervention against the Bolsheviks in the 1919 Russian Civil War, are proudly displayed at several locations in Waterfront Park and are also celebrated in a permanent exhibit at the Oregon Historical Society. In the 1930s, the late Oregon political leader **Monroe Sweetland 76** called the *Oregon* a "propaganda battle-ship" that "glorifies the entirely uncalled-for war against Spain, which Americans should be eager to forget."

Another group of nineteenth-century dissenters chose to establish utopian communities instead of directly challenging industrial capitalism. Agricultural in nature, these communities were located outside the city and were based on common ownership and collective work. But some—none of which survived—were nearby, including the Aurora Colony (1878), **Socialist 5** (1895), Nehalem Valley Cooperative Colony (1886), Bellamy (1897), and, far away in Douglas County, New Odessa (1882).[2] The Byrdcliffe Arts Colony that later became famous in Woodstock, New York, was originally planned by Ralph Radcliffe Whitehead and Hervey White near Alsea in 1901 but was soon abandoned.[3]

Although Oregon's black community numbered only 1,105 in 1900 (of whom about 70 percent resided in Multnomah County) and the state's constitution contained prohibition against black, Chinese, or "mulatto" residence, suffrage, and other civil rights, an **Afro-American League 10** was established in Portland by 1898. Many Portland-rooted black families can trace their histories to the Portland Hotel, which originally hired seventy-five black employees when it opened in 1880, and to the national railroads, which came shortly afterward and made the Pullman porter one of the more secure jobs open to black people.

Early-Portland's race riots were white attacks on Chinese workers. The economic depression of 1884 persuaded some jobless workers and even union organizers that, rather than capitalism, their plight was caused by Chinese workers, originally recruited to build the western railroads. In 1886, white mobs kidnapped one hundred and sixty Chinese workers at the Oregon City Woolen Mills and marched them to the Plaza Blocks. There, a torch-carrying mob of over one thousand white people demanded they leave town.[4]

1 THE SLAVE YORK 🌐

York, the slave that William Clark took on the military/commercial reconnaissance known as the Lewis and Clark Expedition, was commemorated in 2010 with a sculpture at the Watzek Library at Lewis & Clark College. "York: Terra Incognita" was created by artist Alison Saar and depicts one of William Clark's maps engraved on York's back. The monument was the idea of Charles Neal, a black Portlander who also persuaded the City Council to dedicate *NE York Street* in honor of York after research did not disclose for whom the street was originally named. York, who did not take the last name of his owner, was allowed to carry a gun, to hunt, and to vote on where the expedition would spend the winter. Afterwards, however, Clark denied him his freedom, and while other men on the expedition received land for their efforts, York did not. Clark boasted of beating him for being "of very little Service to me [Clark], insolent and Sulky."

2 SOCIALIST LABOR PARTY MEETINGS 🌐

Until quite recently, members of Local Section Portland of the historic SLP still met monthly in the Multnomah County Central Library at *801 SW 10th Avenue*. Outside Portland, Astoria's former SLP hall exists as a mid-century time capsule in the Bergerson Tile and Stone store at *1796 Exchange Street*.[5]

Members of the Socialist Labor Party met monthly at the Multnomah County Library at 801 SW 10th Avenue. *Colin Smith.*

3 MARY LEONARD

The first woman to practice law in Oregon, **Mary Leonard**, finally succeeded in 1886 after a long and hard-fought battle in the State Legislature and Supreme Court. Her legal career was stimulated by the months she spent in the Wasco County jail before being acquitted of murdering her former husband. But her career ended in 1912 when she walked out of court in Portland. She was found ill and alone a few months later in a little house on E. Washington Street and died in the Multnomah County poor farm (now McMenamins Edgefield Manor, *2126 SW Halsey Street* in Troutdale). Her body was donated to the University of Oregon Medical School, today's Oregon Health and Science University.

4 CLARA SHORTRIDGE FOLTZ

Clara Shortridge Foltz (1849–1934), the first woman attorney in California, moved to Portland with her husband around 1864. She stayed for about a year and was a dressmaker before moving back to California. In 1878, she returned to address the Oregon Women's Suffrage Association meeting, just before she passed the bar exam (by "reading"—serving an apprenticeship with an attorney) and was admitted to practice in California.

5 SOCIALIST VALLEY ROAD

Arguably America's only public road commemorating socialism is in Polk County near Portland. **Socialist Valley Road** led from Fall City to Socialist Valley, founded in 1895 as one of the cooperative settlements that flourished briefly in the state. The town sent ten dollars to the Socialist Party as its monthly dues in May 1907, but by 1920 the town was abandoned and nature was retaking its site. The Oregon Department of Transportation also lists the Socialist Valley Bridge, on Socialist Valley Road over the Little Luckiamute River.

6 THE FIFTH REGIMENT OF COXEY'S ARMY 🎤

The Fifth Regiment of Coxey's Army was recruited by local organizer Jack Short at *SW 3rd Avenue and Burnside Street* in 1894, with the support of the Central Labor Council and a contingent of fifty brought up from San Francisco by a Captain Kain—whose "advance party" of four included three black members. A major economic depression had

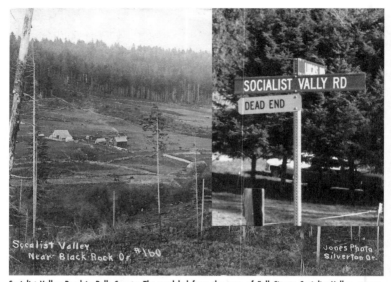

Socialist Valley Road in Polk County. The road led from the town of Fall City to Socialist Valley, a cooperative settlement founded in 1895. It is, arguably, America's only public road commemorating socialism. *Michael Munk.*

inspired an Ohio businessman, Jacob Coxey, to organize a march on Washington by what he called a "United States Industrial Army" to demand hundreds of thousands of road-building jobs for the unemployed. While in Portland, Coxey supporters engaged in furious debate with *The Oregonian*, which called them "a mobilization of bandits [and] a menace to law and order," as well as with the City Board of Charities which regarded them as "organized vagrants for the purpose of terrorizing the community." Kain fired back: "We are starving in a land of plenty. Why?" At one of their rallies held at their camp near the Southern Pacific rail yards, one thousand five hundred Portlanders came out to lend their support.

Intending to take over a train bound for Washington, D.C., the 446 men of the Fifth Regiment now led by stonemason E. F. Schier occupied an eastbound train at the Troutdale depot on April 28, 1894. They were arrested by federal troops 120 miles east of Portland, at Arlington, and returned to Portland in boxcars under heavy guard.[6] A trial, accompanied by downtown rallies with over one thousand supporters, led to their apologies for breaking the law and their release. Most of them apparently left in groups of ten to twenty-five on eastbound freights.

THE FIREBRAND
For the Burning Away of the Cobwebs of Ignorance and Superstition.

VOL. I.   PORTLAND, OREGON, SUNDAY, AUGUST 11, 1895.   NO. 27.

Publication of *The Firebrand*, a national anarchist weekly, was launched in 1895 from the Sellwood neighborhood by Henry Addis, Abner J. Pope, and Abraham Isaak. Publication ceased in 1897 when the three men were arrested and convicted of sending obscene literature through the mail. *Oregon Historical Society, microfilm.*

7 *FIREBRAND*

In 1895, the national anarchist weekly **Firebrand** was launched from a farm in Portland's Sellwood neighborhood by Henry Addis, farmer and former SLP member, Abner J. Pope, scion of a prominent New England Quaker family, and Russian immigrant Abraham Isaak — supported by Mary Isaak's laundry work. *Firebrand* first appeared in January with the goal of filling in a perceived gap in Portland's local papers. Addis explained:

> *A little over a year ago comrade [J. H.] Morris was running a small job printing office in this city. Comrades Mary Squire [corset maker], A. Isaak, Ezekiel Slabs [gardener], John Pawson [woodcutter] and myself visited the meetings in the city where free discussion was had, and occasionally took part in the discussions. We also tried to get our ideas into the local "reform" press. We finally found all the columns of the press closed against us, except on condition that we "trim" our contributions. We talked the matter over and concluded to start a paper.[7]*

The early issues of the paper reflect this localized radical or reform community, including announcements for Portland's Secular Union, events at the German **Turn Verein Hall 182**, Knights of Labor union meetings, Spiritualists, and the Central Labor Union. But the paper quickly adopted a more militant anarchist outlook and established itself as not just for Portland, or even the West, but also for the whole Anarchist Movement.

Publication ended in 1897 when the three men were arrested and convicted on federal charges of sending obscene literature (a Walt Whitman poem) through the mail. After their release from prison, Mary Isaak later traveled with the anarchist leader and *Firebrand* contributor **Emma Goldman 33**. Addis had arranged for one of Goldman's earliest visits to Portland in 1898, and in 1899 after her Portland lecture, Goldman visited Scio (founded by Czechs), where she met Gertie Vose, Donald Vose's mother, and the town marshal offered her use of city hall.

Herman Eich, a Jewish German immigrant called Portland's "rag-picker poet," wrote many of the poems that appeared on the front page of every issue of the paper, including "The Red Flag," which appeared in the second issue, "Freedom," which appeared on September 6, 1896, together with his obituary, and "Another Victim," by J. H. Morris. Eich, about thirty-two, was killed riding the rods to promote the *Firebrand* in the east when a Union Pacific brakeman ordered him off a moving freight car in Rock Springs, Wyoming. He fell and was crushed under the wheels.[8]

8 THE EQUAL SUFFRAGE ASSOCIATION ☻

The Equal Suffrage Association, organized in 1896, had its first office at 294 *SW Clay Street*. Speakers that year included county Judge J. A. Ward, who was welcomed as "another one of the manly men who are in perfect accord with their wives and daughters as advocates of equal rights for all people," and the learned Dr. Jinda Ram who spoke on the Hindu philosophy "from conception to cremation." Later, the Equal Suffrage office relocated to the Selling Building (today's Oregon National Building) at 610 *SW Alder Street*, and remained there until World War I.

9 LOWNSDALE SQUARE ☻

Despite opposition from the local Anti-Imperialist League, the 1898 U.S. invasion and occupation of the Philippines and Cuba are celebrated by several monuments in the heart of downtown Portland. The oldest is in **Lownsdale Square** between the Multnomah County Courthouse and the Mark O. Hatfield U.S. Courthouse; it honors the Second Oregon Volunteer Infantry Regiment's participation in the war against Filipino independence. Ironically, this monument soon became the favorite gathering place for the early Wobblies and in the 1930s for the Communists' May Day demonstrations.[9]

Lownsdale Square, between today's Multnomah County Courthouse and the Mark O. Hatfield U.S. Courthouse, was a favorite gathering place for Portland's radicals. This photo, taken at a Communist Party gathering, shows the monument to the Second Oregon Volunteer Infantry's involvement in the U.S. occupation of the Philippines and Guam in 1898. *City of Portland Archives, A2001-074.4.*

During the war for the Philippines, **Charles Erskine Scott (C. E. S.) Wood** 41 expressed his solidarity with the Filipino Resistance in a prominent western magazine published in Portland. "Were I a Filipino [and found that the United States] came with hammer and sword, not to strike off my shackles, but to rivet them faster," he wrote, "I would fight, fight, fight till the sun was blotted from my eyes."[10]

10 AFRO-AMERICAN LEAGUE 🌐

At its hall at *SW 2nd Avenue and Yamhill Street* in November 1898, Portland's **Afro-American League** held a mass meeting to protest a white terrorist attack on the elected city government of Wilmington, North Carolina, whose officials were mostly black; J. N. Fullilove (a barber who lived at *1732 SE Morrison Street*), Rev. Shepard S. Freeman of the Bethel African Methodist Episcopal Church (then at *226 NW 10th Avenue*; Freeman lived at *314 Everett Street*), and E. McGee spoke. A petition to President McKinley was adopted proclaiming that "the colored citizens of Portland, Oregon…protest against the massacre and unlawful treatment accorded Afro-Americans in the city of Wilmington, N. C. and as many more in Greenwood, S. C."[11] In 2006, an 1898 Wilmington Race Riot Commission issued a report noting the racist attack in Wilmington in which an unknown number of black people were killed and many others forced to flee as the "only successful overthrow of a municipal government in American history," and laid the foundation for voter disenfranchisement in North Carolina.[12] In March 1900, "in a new departure for Oregon politics, thirty-four young men" signed up with the Negro Democratic Club at *82 NE 2nd Street* and elected C. A. Hughes president, Grant Cross vice president, G. W. Hamilton secretary, and Pendleton Smith treasurer.

THE NINETEENTH CENTURY NOTES

1. For meeting details, visit the Portland **SLP** website at http://slp.pdx.home.mindspring.com.

2. James J. Kopp, "Documenting Utopia in Oregon," *Oregon Historical Quarterly*, Summer 2004.

3. "After a scandalous affair with a Miss Hart in California, Whitehead in 1901 enlisted the help of the writer Hervey White to help him plan another ideal commune. They chose a site near Albany, Oregon, in a spot so remote that self-sufficiency was the only way to stay alive. A group of musicians was dispatched in the fall to build the colony, by the time White and Whitehead arrived the following July, the settlers were all quarreling and the commune was abandoned before it began." Robert Edwards, "The Utopias of Ralph Radcliffe Whitehead," *Antiques* 1985.

4. In the 1970s, the Portland Labor Players produced a re-enactment of the story called *Season of Silence: Life and Labor in the Oregon City Woolen Mills.*

5. Astoria is also the birthplace of the famous radical photographer Consuelo Kanaga (1894–1978). She was the daughter of Clatsop County District Attorney Amos Kanaga and writer Mathilde Hartwig Kanaga. The family left Oregon for San Francisco around 1900, where Consuelo later began a career that took her around the world to document the class struggle. *She is a Tree of Life to Them* in the celebrated *1955 Family of Man* exhibition is one of the best-known photographs by a native Oregonian.

6. Dmitri Palmateer, "Charity and the 'Tramp': Itinerancy, Unemployment, and Municipal Government from Coxey to the Unemployed League," *Oregon Historical Quarterly*, Summer 2006.

7. Carlos Schwantes, "Free Love and Free Speech on the Pacific Northwest Frontier: Proper Victorians vs. Portland's 'Filthy' *Firebrand*," *Oregon Historical Quarterly*, Fall 1981.

8. For more on Eich, see Paul Avrich's *Anarchist Portraits* (Princeton: Princeton University Press, 1990).

9. Sean McEnroe, "Painting the Philippines with an American Brush: Visions of Race and National Mission among the Oregon Volunteers in the Philippine Wars of 1898 and 1899," *Oregon Historical Quarterly*, Spring 2003.

10. Charles Erskine Scott (C. E. S.) Wood, "Imperialism and Democracy," *Pacific Monthly*, June 1899.

11. *The Oregonian*, November 18, 1898.

12. *The New York Times*, June 3, 2006.

Utopians & Marxists Downtown

CHAPTER TWO

WOBBLIES & SOCIALISTS

1900–1930

William U'Ren defended members of the Portland Communist Labor Party against charges of violating the state Criminal Syndicalism Act on March 10, 1920. U'Ren (middle-right) is flanked by the defendants, (from left) Claud Hurst, Fred W. Fry, and Karl W. Oster. Hurst was sentenced to two years in prison, Fry was given parole (he was deaf), and Oster was sentenced to five years in prison. *Oregon Historical Society, CN009663.*

During the first three decades of the twentieth century, the radicals of the previous century were followed by mass movements that more specifically offered the alternatives of Socialism and, after the Russian Revolution, Communism. The largest of these was the Socialist Party led by Eugene Debs. The Socialist Party was committed to electoral participation by urban workers and was most successful in rural areas. In 1900, Oregon's Socialist Party polled only one thousand five hundred votes, while William Jennings Bryan's Democratic People's Party had a total of thirty-three thousand. But when Debs brought his campaign to Oregon in 1908, he drew large crowds and inspired radicals like Eugene's Floyd Ramp (1874–1973) to a lifetime of revolutionary commitment.

> *Ten thousand persons at the Exposition Building last night heard Eugene V. Debs, Socialist nominee for President, excoriate the Republicans and Democrats as the instrument of the capitalist class. The demonstration that attended Mr. Deb's appearance in the Exposition building was remarkable. The instant the Socialist leader entered the hall, the signal was given and the band started up a lively air. Simultaneously the entire audience arose as one man and with shouts that shook the rafters of the building greeted their chief.*
> — *The Oregonian*, September 15, 1908

Debs came to Portland on his campaign train, "The Red Special" with the "Red Special Band." The three-story Exposition Building stood on the north side of what is today PGE Park.

More than 10 percent of Oregon's voters (thirteen thousand) supported Debs for President on the Socialist Party ticket in 1912, with his strongest support not in Portland but in rural Josephine, Jackson, and Coos counties where he came in second. That high-water mark for the Socialist Party was also the year when a Socialist from St. Johns was elected city alderman in Portland, and socialists were elected as the mayor of Coquille and a councilman in Medford.

The number of Portland Socialist Party locals rose from five in 1907, when they joined the **Industrial Workers of the World (IWW)** 17 march to celebrate the acquittal of Wobbly leader William "Big Bill" Haywood, to nine in 1919. Six of those locals were foreign-language based. A Multnomah County Local of the Socialist Party still meets at the Belmont Library, *1038 SE Cesar E. Chavez Boulevard.*[1]

The IWW, whose members were called Wobblies, was another radical working-class organization. However, unlike the Socialist Party, the IWW expressed contempt for electoral politics. Instead, it was committed to replacing capitalism by organizing the working class into one big union that, when strong enough, would refuse to work for capitalists and bring down the system. In 1907, in one of their first strikes anywhere, local Wobblies organized three thousand sawmill workers to walk out of Portland's saw mills and demand higher wages and shorter hours. In 1913, another Wobbly-supported strike, this time against the **Oregon Packing Company** 24, inspired some Portlanders to become prominent radicals, including **Dr. Marie Equi** 16 and **Tom Burns** 70.

The Oregon system of electoral initiative, referendum, and recall is an enduring child of the populist movement. In 1902, Oregon voters passed William U'Ren's direct legislation package based on support from the rural Grange and the labor movement. His People's Power League (1905) continued the struggle for clean government as they charged Portland's business leaders with widespread vice and corruption. A mayoral commission in 1912 listed 431 properties as "wholly given up to immorality." Their owners were well-known local "community leaders," including members of the Ainsworth Failing, Corbett, Reed, Weinhard, and Glisan families.[2]

Limits on dissent were systematically imposed on opponents of the United States entry into World War I and continued after the war with the federal government's notorious Palmer Raids, jailing and deporting many radicals. In support of the Red Scare, the Oregon legislature passed the Criminal Syndicalism Act. The Portland Police Bureau established its infamous **Red Squad** 194, developed from a "reserve squad" originally created in 1914 to enforce Portland's vagrancy and vice statutes. By World War I, however, its scope had been expanded to include anti-radical activities.[3] The ban on "vagrants" (defined as anyone having less than five dollars or so in their pockets) reflected the fact that great numbers of single men moved throughout the country during that era looking for work. In one of their songs, already well known by 1910, an Irish worker reflects unfavorably on his experiences in our "Portland County Jail." Between 1900 and 1939, the Multnomah County Jail was at Kelly Butte where prisoners pounded rocks in a quarry.

> I'm a stranger in your city,
> My name is Paddy Flynn;
> I got drunk the other evening,
> And the coppers run me in.

> I had no money to pay my fine,
> No friends to go my bail;
> So I got soakt for 90 days
> In the Portland County Jail.

More recently, the jail was honored with the "Rocky Butte Blues" by Delmark Goldfarb, who protested a shorter sentence.

> The judge he told me
> I'd better change my ways
> And then he slapped me down
> And give me sixty days.

> I just don't know what I'm going to do
> I'm going to Rocky Butte
> I'm going to Rocky Butte
> I'm going to Rocky Butte Jail.

All three levels of government soon organized raids, mass arrests, vigilante assaults, and deportations of radical Portland groups, including

Wobblies, Socialists, labor organizers, and antiwar agitators. U'Ren himself defended some of those arrested.

At the same time, the Russian Revolution (chronicled by Portland's best-known radical, **John Reed** 31, in his *Ten Days That Shook the World*) set off a fresh surge of radical activity, including the organization of a Portland Soviet modeled after the Russian Soviets, and several varieties of a Communist Party.

The last major electoral effort of the populists came in 1924 when Robert M. LaFollette Jr.'s Progressive Party, a coalition similar to the earlier populists, came in second in Oregon with 25 percent of the vote — which now included women — and captured almost a third of the votes in the Portland area.

11 WILLIAM Z. FOSTER 🌐

Former W. Burnside Street saloons are the sites associated with **William Z. Foster** (1881–1961), labor leader and longtime head of the U.S. Communist Party. He made Portland his home beginning in 1901, hoboing here until 1907. He worked in lumber camps, laid railroad track along the Columbia River near White Salmon, and shoveled heavy green railroad ties on the Portland docks, where he joined the Longshoremen's Union. Soon after his arrival, he shipped out for several years and returned to Portland in 1904 (just in time, he said, to join 7,618 other male Oregonians to vote for Socialist Party presidential candidate Eugene Debs). With his brother-in-law George McVey, he claimed three hundred and twenty acres (and a timber claim the same size) in the Mosier homesteads, calling it "a wild country, heavily timbered and full of fish and game, back of the famous Hood River apple district...south of the Great Columbia River...in the background loomed magnificent Mount Hood." After three summers, he gave up the land and ended what he called "the first and last time in my life that I ever attempted to gather together property."[4] After voting for Debs, Foster formalized his ties to radical politics by joining a Portland local of the Socialist Party, reading Marxist classics, and selling socialist newspapers in the streets. The Socialist Party's leader in Portland was Tom Sladen, whom Foster described as "a champion of working class culture who considered cuspidors 'bourgeois' and removed them from the party office." Foster also recalls the government kidnapping of IWW leader "Big Bill" Haywood and was probably among the three thousand workers who marched to protest in the IWW's first Portland demonstration

Erickson's Saloon was a favorite of William Z. Foster, labor leader and longtime head of the U.S. Communist Party. *Colin Smith.*

The plaque on the building that once housed Erickson's reads: "Loggers, farmhands, and other robust working men came to Erickson's, some to spend their stakes in one night revelries, buying drinks all around." *Colin Smith.*

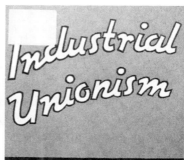

This pamphlet of Foster's on Industrial Unionism, published in 1936, sold for five cents. *Oregon Historical Society, PAM 331.88 F758i.*

BY
WM. Z. FOSTER

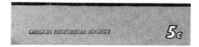

on February 24, 1907. Five Socialist Party Locals joined forty of the sixty labor unions in the city that day.

During his Portland years, Foster frequented Skid Road bars, including Erickson's Saloon (recently the Barracuda nightclub) at *9 NW 2nd Avenue*. A sign above its entrance read, "A Workingmen's Club Known as Erickson's" well into the 1960s, but Foster's favorite hangout was across the street at the former Brazier Brothers Saloon, now *222 W. Burnside Street*. He recounts that the Brazier was so well known that on a railroad water tank at The Dalles, "I once read the following realistic poetic outburst of an eastbound hobo returning from the Pacific Coast."[5]

> I came out West for change and rest;
> But the whores got my change,
> And Brazier got the rest.

12 ANNIVERSARY OF THE EMANCIPATION PROCLAMATION

The Afro-American League 10 held its annual celebration of the anniversary of the Emancipation Proclamation on New Year's Day 1902, at the AME Zion Church, *1229 SW Main Street*. This celebration "consisted of several musical numbers and addresses."

13 1905 LEWIS AND CLARK EXHIBITION PROTEST

Construction of Portland's Lewis and Clark Centennial and American Pacific Exposition and Oriental Fair in March of 1905 began with a picket line at its gates at *NW 25th Avenue and Vaughn Street* — an episode rarely noted in the celebratory histories of the event. At the time, *The Oregonian* found twenty-five pickets "chosen at a large meeting of workmen, following upon an unsuccessful attempt of agitators to call a general strike." Their demands were "not to be compelled to work with any but union men, recognition of their unions and an eight hour day." While the account hopefully predicted that "the pickets are not likely to be successful," it understood "the fact that all men hate to be called scabs" as "the only strong weapon in the hands of the pickets."[6]

14 HARRY LANE

A son of one of Oregon's prominent pioneers, **Harry Lane, MD**, was elected mayor of Portland in 1905 with working-class support and business elite opposition. He energetically exposed the long-standing practice of granting municipal franchises to political contributors. A city that "voluntarily consents to being assessed and taxed by a private corporation," he declared, "is unfit to exist." But Lane's vetoes of the city council's giveaways were usually overridden and, like many reformers, he failed to end municipal corruption. Elected to the U.S. Senate in 1912, his anti-imperialist stance led him to become one of only six senators to oppose United States entry into World War I, an opinion for which his enemies savagely attacked him. He died a month after that vote. His daughter Nina was a Socialist and married her comrade Issac McBridge, who became Lane's secretary in the Senate. Lane is buried in Lone Fir Cemetery on *SE 23rd Avenue and Stark Street*, where, in 1940, the Portland Peace Day Conference held a service in his memory.

The White Eagle Saloon, now owned by local restaurant chain McMenamins, was named for the Polish national symbol. It hosted the radical Polish group Progress in rooms upstairs. *McMenamins.*

15 WHITE EAGLE SALOON 🍷

Today's popular music venue, the **White Eagle Saloon** at *836 N. Russell Street*, was named for the Polish national symbol when it opened in 1906, and a radical Polish group, Progress, was meeting in rooms upstairs. Reactionary local Poles falsely accused Progress of being anarchists plotting to assassinate President William Howard Taft.[7] That was enough for the Portland police and the Secret Service to raid the saloon shortly after it opened.

Dr. Marie D. Equi was one of the first women to graduate from the University of Oregon Medical School in 1903. She also fought militantly for workers' and women's rights. *Oregon Historical Society, OrHi60822.*

The house where Dr. Marie D. Equi lived with Elizabeth Gurley Flynn is located at 1423 SW Hall Street. *Colin Smith.*

16 DR. MARIE D. EQUI 🌹

One of the first women to graduate from the University of Oregon Medical School (1903), **Dr. Marie D. Equi** (1872–1952) is best known for her lifelong struggle for workers' and women's rights. After setting up her medical practice, which included abortion services to both working-class and high-society women, she lived with her assistant, Harriet Speckert, in what is today's Mark Spencer Hotel (then the Nortonia Hotel) at *409 SW 11th Avenue*. Radicalized by police suppression of **Oregon Packing Company women strikers** 24 in 1913, Equi was an outspoken opponent of United States entry into World War I, famously confronting Portland's 1916 Preparedness Day parade with a banner proclaiming "Down with Imperialism." On May Day 1916, Equi was selected as Oregon's representative to scatter Wobbly martyr **Joe Hill's** 19 ashes (after his execution, his ashes were divided into forty-seven packets and one was sent to labor leaders in every state — except Utah, where he was murdered). She was arrested many times in struggles over birth control, labor, and peace. Finally, as punishment for making an antiwar speech at the IWW Hall in June 1918, she was sentenced to three years in San Quentin State Prison, despite being defended by **Colonel Charles Erskine Scott (C. E. S.) Wood** 41. The federal government employed Margaret Lowell Paul as an informer against Equi during the Irish nationalist Kathleen O'Brennan's visit to Portland. In the Portland Hotel in August of 1918, Equi confronted U.S. military intelligence agents who were harassing O'Brennan. Equi was able to trigger a police raid on the hotel as a site of prostitution, telling the manager it was in retaliation for his cooperation with the intelligence agents.

Equi's longtime housemate at *1433 SW Hall Street*, Communist leader **Elizabeth Gurley Flynn** 53, recalled the following: "Doctor [Equi] gets [liquor] from the police station…the big cops come sneaking up with it for her." In poor health, Equi left her bed for the first time in two years in July 1934 to take a check for $250 to striking longshoremen in order to assure their medical care.

For May Day, 1950, radical activist **Julia Ruuttila** 175 was asked by Portland longshore leader **Francis Murnane** 171 to write a poem for Dr. Equi. As late as the early years of McCarthyism, an earlier custom persisted among radical men to present red roses to the women in their lives, as Murnane and fellow longshoremen delivered to Equi with this poem:

> *To Dr. Marie Equi, May Day, 1950,*
> These are for you, thirteen red roses, Doc;
> Your lucky number in the old cell block
> Chalked on cold stone. This day is ours
> To honor heroes, mark the labor gain.
> We who have suffered have our special flowers,
> Deep as our blood and dark with Portland rain.
> Thirteen red roses.
>
> Jack London and Tom Paine,
> Haywood and Everest, Frank Little and Joe Hill,
> Pat Carr and Mooney, all the Ludlow dead,
> Gene Debs, Joe Johnson and Jim Ray,
> Becker and Bridges. Labor's blood was red
> at Boston Common; when the Verona fell,
> On the Embarcadero with the maritime dead;
> In South Chicago with a storm of lead.
> Workers and martyrs.
>
> Doc, your coat lapel
> Must wear a rose for us on labor's day.
> Fighter and friend to valiant end,
> Our champion to revere and defend,
> Wear roses for us, Doc, this First of May.

She adopted Mary Equi (1915–1998), who became the youngest female pilot in the Northwest in 1932 and later married the radical Joseph C. Lukes, a 1934 Reed College graduate. A play dramatizing the relations between Equi, Flynn, and Mary, *A Most Dangerous Woman* by Myra Donnelly, was produced at the Interstate Firehouse Cultural Center in Portland in 1995.

Equi died in 1952 at Fairlawn Hospital.

17 INDUSTRIAL WORKERS OF THE WORLD ✿

IWW, whose members were known as the Wobblies, was a dedicated enemy of capitalism and received significant support from workers who believed they should rule the world. Unlike the Socialist Party, the IWW expressed contempt for electoral politics. In Portland and throughout the Northwest, the IWW attracted loggers, miners, farmhands, and mill workers, renting its first Portland hall at *493 W. Burnside Street* in 1907. They later moved to *NW 2nd Avenue and Couch Street* and then to *535 NW Davis Street* — a site recently replaced by a fashionable condo. In March 1907, the IWW conducted its first major strike when one thousand six hundred men, organized by W. Y. Yarrow, struck the Eastern & Western Lumber Mill on the north waterfront of McCormick Pier and the Inman-Poulsen Mill on the east side, between the Hawthorne and Ross Island Bridges. Three thousand sawmill workers walked out of the mills, demanding higher wages and shorter hours. The Wobblies called this "the first shot in the class war in the Northwest." Resurrected late in the twentieth century, the Wobblies have made several more recent attempts to organize gas stations, restaurants, child welfare centers, and the Reed College library in Portland. In 2006, their hall was at *311 N. Ivy Street*.

The Wobblies were a major target of reactionary vigilantes, local police, and the federal government. During World War I, timber barons and the federal government organized the "Loyal Legion of

CHAPTER TWO:
Wobblies & Socialists

The building at 222-24 W. Burnside served as headquarters for the IWW during the early years of the organization's life in Portland. *City of Portland Archives A2000-033.*

Loggers and Lumbermen" to fight the Wobblies in the Northwest forests. Their Oregon leader was Norman Coleman, later president of Reed College. When Florence vigilantes kidnapped seven Wobblies in 1913, Governor Oswald D. West considered imposing martial law on the town. IWW members were also among the first victims of Oregon's notorious Criminal Syndicalism Act[8], which was Salem's answer to the

This IWW poster's heading, "Education—Organization—Emancipation," represents the most basic strategy used by the IWW in their struggle to give power to the "working class," which they tried to form into "one big union." *Oregon Historical Society, OrHi77730.*

Russian Revolution and became the legal foundation for the ensuing Red Scare. The law was first used by the Portland Police **Red Squad 194** to arrest Wobbly Jay Wirth for selling the IWW newspaper on the street in 1919. On November 11, 1919, **The Council of Workers, Soldiers, and Sailors 43** was raided and fifty-six people, including twenty-six Wobblies, were arrested. Less than two months later, about thirty members of the Communist Labor Party (CLP)—which **John Reed 31** had recently helped organize—were arrested. The twenty-six Wobblies and six of the CLP members were charged with violating the Criminal Syndicalism Act, which the CLP called the "Oregon Comical Silliyism Law," and about twelve received deportation warrants. William U'Ren defended three of the CLP members but one of them, writing from the Multnomah County Jail, complained that U'Ren had only read Tennyson poems to the jury and "absolutely forgot to refute any of the accusations of the prosecution. In short, he sabotaged on us all the way through."⁹

The last Wobbly prosecuted under the act was Ole Hendricks, arrested in Tillamook in 1923 and defended by Portland progressive attorney **Burl (B. A.) Green 73**. Hendricks's trial ended in a hung jury, but the act was used against other radicals, mainly Communists such as **Ben Boloff 50**. This ended in 1938 when the U.S. Supreme Court freed Portland Communist leader **Dirk DeJonge 63** from prison.

In May of 1912, Wobblies organized a brief strike of five hundred tracklayers to protest the Portland Railway, Light, and Power Company's corrupt job-fee racket. In 1914, they invented the eat-in. Forty Wobblies entered Meves Restaurant at *SW 6th Avenue and Washington Street*, ordered bountiful meals, and told the cashier that Mayor Albee would pay for it. A crowd of five hundred watched from the sidewalk as twenty police arrived to remove the well-fed Wobblies, who were then sentenced to jail. The same day, fourteen Wobblies ate at Peerless Cafeteria, and the next day, seven ate steaks at another restaurant.

At the Spanish-American War Monument in **Lownsdale Square 9**, the IWW held a free speech rally on the evening of July 17, 1913. This rally was attacked by angry veterans, who were deputized as specials by the city, and about twenty-five Wobblies were jailed. Their comrades then demonstrated before the neighboring Multnomah County Courthouse, demanding the release of fellow worker George Reece and other Wobblies.

18 ED BOYCE 🌐

Ed Boyce, a leader of the Western Federation of Miners in Idaho and a supporter of the **IWW** 17 and Eugene Debs, moved to Portland in 1909 after retiring from union organizing. Here, he "became an avid reader of social theory and Irish poetry" and lived quietly with his wife Eleanor, "often passing the whole day sitting in the same room reading." Eleanor took an interest in art and became a member of the Portland Art Association, and the family donated freely to a number of local charities. In 1911, Boyce invested money in the Portland Hotel, then located at the current site of *Pioneer Square*, and other local real estate and was elected president of the Oregon Hotel Association in 1936. When he died in 1941, the former radical left an estate of over $1 million, and perhaps that's why after Boyce moved to Portland, Debs wrote that he had been "virtually forgotten by the officials of the organization he served at a time when it required real men to speak out for labor."

19 JOE HILL 🌐

In late 1910, the Wobbly organizer and songwriter **Joe Hill** wrote a letter to *The Industrial Worker*, the IWW newspaper, identifying himself as a member of the Portland IWW Local, signing the first documented use of the name (his Swedish name was Hillstrom) which would later become known throughout the world. He mentioned traveling through Pendleton and denounced Portland police attacks on Wobblies and other workers in the Portland area. Hill rose in the IWW organization and traveled widely, organizing workers under the IWW banner, writing political songs and satirical poems, and making speeches until he was murdered (executed by firing squad) by the state of Utah in 1915. His ashes were divided into forty-seven packets and sent to radicals in every state except Utah "to be scattered to the winds." In Oregon, **Dr Marie Equi 16** was given the honor. One of his best-known songs, "The Preacher and the Slave" (a parody of the then well-known hymn "In the Sweet Bye and Bye"), was first introduced in Portland shortly after his letter was published in 1910. Another Wobbly songmaster, Harry "Haywire Mac" McClintock, recalls, "I first met [Joe Hill] in Portland, Oregon, fall of 1910. He brought 'Preacher and the Slave' to the Portland IWW Hall,"[10] then on *W. Burnside and SW Third Avenue*. It has appeared in every edition of the IWW's *Little Red Songbook* since 1911 as "Long-haired Preacher Man."

Joe Hill Night is Portland's tribute to the IWW songwriter and the labor movement he represented. This flier advertised the 2006 version of this party, which was held at Liberty Hall in North Portland. There was a radical book fair and music from local radical bands. *Portland IWW.*

Long-haired Preacher Man

Long-haired preachers come out every night,
Try to tell you what's wrong and what's right;
But when asked how 'bout something to eat
They will answer with voices so sweet:
You will eat, bye and bye
In that glorious land above the sky;
Work and pray,
Live on hay,
You'll get pie in the sky when you die

20 MARCH OF THE UNEMPLOYED 1914

On January 11, 1914, Wobblies joined an "army of the unemployed" and marched from Portland down the Willamette Valley. Oregon City's mayor let 125 marchers use its armory and fed them supper and breakfast. By contrast, the mayor of Woodburn organized a posse of several hundred men to keep the marchers from stopping in town. In Salem they camped outside Governor Oswald D. West's home. West was sympathetic, but he did not succeed in persuading the legislature to pass a public works bill. A few of the marchers got jobs through Salem churches, but more were arrested in the **IWW's** 17 restaurant "eat-in" and expelled from town. Albany's mayor ordered his fire department to threaten the Wobblies with fire hoses, but the march continued down to Eugene.

21 KATHRYN SEAMAN BECK 🌐

Kathryn (Kitty) Seaman Beck, described as a ward of **Colonel C. E. S. Wood** 41, was actually his lover. She was from a wealthy family and "at home in the world of literature, art, philosophy, and biography." She was Wood's secretary in his private office in room 419 of the Chamber of Commerce building, *525 SW 5th Avenue*, and ran the Portland defense committee for the IWW leadership on trial for sedition in 1919. Observing the trial in Chicago, she met George Vanderveer, a prominent attorney who headed their defense and later opened a Legal Aid Bureau in Portland. She became his close companion and later, his wife. Shortly after a visit from Wood to their home near Seattle in 1924, the unhappy and drinking Beck committed suicide by inhaling chloroform.[11] **Dr. Equi** 16 accused Wood of being responsible.[12]

22 THE CATLIN-GABEL SCHOOL 🌐

The Catlin-Gabel School, today located at *8825 SW Barnes Road*, was founded in 1911 as Miss Catlin's School for Girls by Ruth Catlin (1883–1978) in a house on NW Irving Street. Committed to the "independence and freedom of action for women," her school drew its students largely from Portland's wealthy elite. She was later placed on a list of active communist sympathizers by the Portland Police **Red Squad** 194 because in 1936 she was a member of the Oregon Committee to Aid Spanish Democracy, which was devoted to defending the elected Spanish government against a fascist invasion. After leaving the school to a board of trustees in 1928, she "took up the cause of workers' rights…and debated with high-powered capitalists."

23 BILLY WEBB ELKS LODGE & YWCA 🌐

Billy Webb Elks Lodge at *6 N. Tillamook Street* was originally a segregated branch of the YWCA for black women. It was established in 1902 because Oregon's white women's clubs had voted to exclude black women from their organizations. In 1926, the city attorney overruled white objections and ordered a building permit be issued for a permanent structure, which became the Williams Avenue Branch of the YWCA or, simply, "the Colored YWCA." The money came from E. S. Collins, a white woman who chaired the YWCA's Committee of Color, although a false rumor circulated that it had come from the Ku Klux Klan to support segregation. Over the years, it was used by a variety of community organizations, and in 1935 a bronze plaque of appreciation to Mrs. Collins "From the Negro Citizens of Portland" was placed in the building.

The Y grew to over 1,000 members by World War II, when it was turned over to the United Service Organization (USO) as a center for black servicemen and women that showcased local black musicians. The Portland NAACP had their office in the basement. But when the USO returned the building to the Y in 1947, efforts to develop interracial programs floundered against a postwar racist backlash. The black community was also shattered by the destruction of much of its housing stock and business property through projects like the Coliseum and Emanuel Hospital's aborted expansion. However, it played a major role after the 1948 Vanport flood, serving as a refuge and soup kitchen for displaced and homeless people.

In 1958, one of the victims of urban renewal was Fraternal Hall at *1412 N. Williams*, which had served as home to several black groups and was used for meetings of the leftist Progressive Party and Civil Rights Congress. So Elks Lodge #1050, affiliated with the "Improved" (colored) Benevolent and Protective Order of Elks of the World since 1906, bought the YWCA building in 1959. They named it for Billy Webb, a pianist member of the Lodge who played in a colored Elks quartet on steamships between Portland and San Francisco in the early 1920s.

By 2008, the building had fallen into disrepair and the National Association of Minority Contractors of Oregon pitched in to help the Elks rehabilitate it.[13]

24 OREGON PACKING COMPANY STRIKE 1913 🎤

The intersection of *SE 7th Avenue and Belmont Street* was the scene of the **1913 Oregon Packing Company Strike**, which was comprised of mainly women workers supported by the **IWW** 17 and other labor organizers. **Dr. Equi** 16 and **Tom Burns** 70, among others, were radicalized by their support of the strike, which was also supported by Portlander Mary

Schwab, a Socialist Party member and daughter-in-law of Chicago Haymarket defendant Michael Schwab. Lucy Parsons, widow of another defendant who was executed for the 1886 bomb attack that killed several policemen, visited Portland to support the strike and to speak at a downtown rally.

The Colored YWCA

Originally the segregated YMCA for black women when it was built in 1926, it was later bought by the "improved" (black) Elks and is now their Billy Webb lodge, named for a pianist member. *Oregon Historical Society, OrHi 87975.*

25 WILL DALY

Everyone expected Portland labor leader and City Council member **Will Daly** (1869–1924) to be elected mayor in 1917. But a few days before the election, *The Oregonian* published on its front page his 1910 application for membership in the Socialist Party (stolen in a burglary the night before). Despite *The Oregonian's* red-baiting, George L. Baker beat Daly by less than two thousand of the forty-eight thousand votes cast, in one of the earliest elections in which women were allowed to vote (the first was Portland's 1913 municipal election). Daly first worked in Portland as a printer, and by 1908 was elected president of the Oregon Federation of Labor.[14] In that position, Daly introduced the IWW's leader, "Big Bill" Haywood, to thousands in a 1909 labor parade as "the man who has suffered more in the cause of organized labor than any other in the U.S.," expressing appreciation for the large Socialist participation in the event. But after he was elected to the city council in 1911, at the urging of the Workingmen's Political Club, he began to distance himself from Socialism.

This did not prevent *The Oregonian* from leading a hysterical campaign against Daly, accusing him of supporting a general strike and asking, "Shall Portland be turned over to the radical labor agitator and the IWW?" Trumpeting his Socialist Party application, the paper tried to frighten its readers by warning, "If the people elect Daly, we shall have a Socialist for mayor." By 1920, Daly's Socialist politics had degenerated to the extent that he endorsed Baker's reactionary administration.

26 SISTER MIRIAM THERESA

Sister Miriam Theresa (born Caroline Gleason, 1886–1962), who co-founded the Catholic Women's League and the Oregon Consumer League, went on to become head of the Social Work department at what today is *Marylhurst University*, south of Portland. Although not an ideological radical, Gleason worked in Portland factories to gather data on the exploitation of women workers, leading to Oregon's enactment of the nation's first effective minimum wage law for women in 1912. As secretary of the Oregon Industrial Welfare Commission, she surveyed living conditions for women in Portland that resulted in a new city housing code. In 1916, she took vows and joined the Sisters of Holy Names and became Sister Miriam Theresa. She went on to become the first woman to receive a PhD from the Catholic University of America. In the tradition of progressive Catholic concern for the working class, she saw the minimum wage law as a means of industrial conciliation between the opposed interests of capital and labor.

27 LOUISE OLIVEREAU 🌎

Louise Olivereau (1884–1963) was associated with the Portland Modern School in 1912. An anarchist, poet, and teacher, she was a typist for the IWW in Seattle when she was convicted and jailed for more than two years (from 1917 to 1920) for opposing World War I. Right after her

release from prison, she spoke at the 1920 May Day rally at Portland's
Finnish Hall 182 at *3425 N. Montana Avenue.*

28 ROUBAIX DE L'ABRIE RICHEY

Roubaix de L'Abrie (Robo) Richey (1890–1922), artist and first husband
of the celebrated photographer and Communist Tina Modotti (1896–
1942), was born on a farm near Portland, attended Lincoln High School,
and studied Spanish at the YMCA. In 1912, while living with his parents
at *3158 SE 51st Avenue,* he published his first short story, "Webfoot," in
the *Overland Monthly.* The story follows an army recruit from Oregon
who kills a railroad worker during a strike and is in turn killed by

the dead worker's enraged
comrades. The dying webfoot
laments, "he would never gaze
upon Oregon ranges or the red
Yamhill slopes down to the
Willamette again." Richey later
moved to San Francisco, where
he met and married Modotti in
1918. While they lived in Los
Angeles, Richey was a cartoon-
ist and contributing editor for
Gale's *International Journal for
Revolutionary Communism.* The
couple later moved to Mexico
where Richey died of smallpox
in 1922. His gravestone at the
American cemetery in Mexico
City is dedicated *from Modottias
Su Esposa* (his wife).

This pamphlet tells the story of Louise Olivereau's trial in
1917. She was tried for her opposition to World War I.
Oregon Historical Society, PAM 323.4 P2246L.

29 GRACE DE GRAFF

In 1915, **Grace De Graff** (1879–1951), principal of Kenton Elementary
School at *7528 N. Fenwick Avenue,* was one of forty-seven women
led by the prominent social reformer Jane Addams, and the only del-
egate from the American West to attend the founding meeting of the
Women's International League for Peace and Freedom (WILPF) at The Hague.
The meeting was a call to women from around the world to "refuse to

do the work men cannot do because they are busy murdering other men." According to her niece in Portland, De Graff "often revealed local scoundrels for what they were," and so "created quite a stir in her day and was not very popular." A lifelong activist and leader of teacher organizations, De Graff received Upton Sinclair, among others, at her home at *2312 SW Sheffield Avenue*. She issued an appeal "To the Teachers of the World" in 1916 that urged them "to teach the truth to the children under your care so that they may no longer be dazzled and blinded by the glittering lies of militarism." Her niece also recalled that De Graff "championed the cause of the socialist regime back in the thirties. She thought what the Russians were doing was a desirable state of affairs." But she also "thought Aaron Frank was the nicest man,"[15] and was able to persuade him to make generous donations to her project for

GRACE deGRAFF

Grace De Graff was a Kenton school principal and a delegate to the founding of the Women's International League for Peace and Freedom (WILPF) at the Hague after World War I.

Kenton school's poor families. She was invited to the White House by Eleanor Roosevelt in 1932 and to Oregon Governor Douglas McKay's inauguration (he was one of her students) in 1949. Her favorite peace organization, WILPF, continues to be active in Portland with offices at *1819 NW Everett Street*.

30 LOUISE BRYANT 🌱

The celebrated radical writer **Louise Bryant** (1887–1936) lived with her first husband, dentist Paul Trullinger, in a houseboat at the Oregon Yacht Club, and maintained a studio in today's Professional Building at *10331 SW Yamhill Street*. They later lived at *2226 NE 53rd Avenue* as well as *11801 SW Riverwood Road*. She met **John Reed** 31 during his visit to Portland in December 1915 and left her husband and Portland to live with (and

Bryant, right, is shown here in Portland circa 1912. Kina McKelvey, left, was a friend. *Larry Armstrong.*

Louise Bryant lived with her first husband, Portland dentist Paul Trullinger, in this house at 2226 NE 53rd Avenue. *Colin Smith.*

eventually marry) him in New York. Bryant considered Portland "a silly old town" because "it had [Reed's] presence here for weeks without appreciating it."[16] For his part, Reed "couldn't imagine" how Bryant could have "grown into an artist, a poet, and a revolutionary" in "this infertile soil, this spiritual vacuum." Bryant returned to Portland only once, in 1919. Before four thousand people in a new Civic Auditorium (today's Keller Auditorium, renovated in 1968) she demanded the immediate withdrawal of U.S. troops from Siberia, sent by President Wilson to unsuccessfully (in Winston Churchill's words) "strangle the Russian Revolution in its cradle." *The Oregonian* noted that she "flourished a red cape that dared Portland to imagine her political beliefs" but that, otherwise, "Louise has changed little. Aside from her George Sand haircut, she is the same little radicalist and vigorous performer that left Portland three years ago." She is buried in Paris.

31 JOHN REED 🌐

Probably the best known of Portland radicals is the writer, poet, and revolutionary **John Reed** (1886–1920). All that remains of the big house on the hill above the city where he was born are the steps linking the ends of *SW Cedar Street and SW Cactus Drive*. He remembered Cedar Hill as a "lordly grey mansion modeled on a French chateau, with its immense park, its formal gardens, lawns, stables, greenhouses, and glass grape arbor, the tame deer among the trees." Reed's first published work was featured in the May 1902 issue of *The Troubadour*, the student literary magazine of his private high school, the Portland Academy. The final stanza of the poem describes the eighteenth century eruption of Mt. St. Helens and its impact on the Columbia River, written when Jack Reed (as he signed himself) was fifteen years old:

> Thus it was the tribe of Clatsops,
> In the dawn of living beings,
> Was swept almost from existence.
> But across that deep, dark valley,
> Flows a river, broad and lovely.
> To the east the Smoking Mountain
> Robed in Liao's snowy blanket
> Rises smokeless now to heaven,
> Covered with eternal whiteness

Home for the summer of 1909 from Harvard, a sarcastic Reed wrote a girl-friend asking if "Portland [was] still the same giddy bewildering place that [made] people leave New York in the gay season and come out here for fun." Visiting on the death of his father in 1912, Reed predicted he'd "go mad in a year" if he had to live here. On his last visit to his hometown in December 1915, Reed found it "awful beyond words...I don't feel I can talk to a single person here." Reed died of typhus in the Soviet Union after publishing *Ten Days That Shook the World* and remains buried in the revolutionaries' cemetery at the walls of the Kremlin.

The John Reed Memorial Bench can be found in Portland's Washington Park. This poster advertised the dedication of that bench in 2001.
Oregon Cultural Heritage Commission.

To celebrate May Day 2001, the Oregon Cultural Heritage Commission dedicated a bench in memory of Reed overlooking his birthplace near the entrance to Washington Park.

All that remains of John Reed's birthplace are the stone steps linking SW Cactus Drive with SW Cedar Street. This photo shows Reed's house as it looked while owned by his grandparents, Mr. and Mrs. H. Green.
Oregon Historical Society, OrHi80890.

32 CARL & HELEN WALTERS 🌐

A Portland couple, **Carl and Helen Walters**,[17] were **John Reed's** 31 and **Colonel C. E. S. Wood's** 41 favorite local artists, as well as **Louise Bryant's** 30 closest friends in 1915. Reed and Bryant's first date was a dinner at the Walters' studio in the former Labbe building at *SW 1st Avenue and Washington Street*. Carl was, like Louise, a subscription agent for the radical monthly, *The Masses*. The Walterses moved to New York in 1919, where Carl became a prominent ceramicist.

33 EMMA GOLDMAN & BEN REITMAN 🌐

In August of 1915, famed radicals **Emma Goldman and Dr. Ben Reitman** were arrested at the Turn Verein Hall, which stood at the northwest corner of *SW Fourth Avenue and Yamhill Street* where they were speaking for birth control and distributing literature. Goldman was released on $500 bail provided by **C. E. S. Wood 41** and after the police chief proclaimed she would not speak in Portland again, she announced that she would try to speak on the subject of birth control the next day, but Dr. Reitman remained in jail. Goldman and Reitman were convicted and fined $100 on the birth control charge, and when Goldman spoke again, the topic was changed to "The Intermediate Sex (A Discussion of Homosexuality)." The audience included plainclothes police, a deputy district attorney, and a deputy city attorney, but Goldman was not arrested on that occasion. That summer she also presented additional lectures at the Portland Public Library to overflowing crowds. Eventually, Goldman's case was dismissed by Portland Circuit Judge William Gatens who concluded, "There is too much tendency to prudery nowadays."

34 BEATRICE MORROW CANNADY 🌐

A few years after **Beatrice Morrow Cannady** arrived in Portland in 1912, she organized one of the city's first interracial protest events: a movement to ban the nation's favorite, but racist, Ku Klux Klan recruiting film, *Birth of a Nation*. Enthusiastically endorsed by President Woodrow Wilson, the silent movie was credited with helping the Oregon Klan grow into a major political force. When it was shown at the singularly named Blue Mouse Theater at *SW 11th Avenue and Washington Street*, its owner John Hamrick used the occasion to announce his Klan membership.[18] According to Portland civil rights activist Bobbie Nunn, the film was eventually banned in Portland in the 1950s after an effort headed by the National Association for the Advancement of Colored People (NAACP) and the Urban League.[19]

Beatrice moved to Portland to marry Edward D. Cannady and to work with him on the four-page weekly, *Advocate*, which Cannady founded in 1903 with other Portland Hotel employees. The Cannadys and their two sons lived at *2516 NE 26th Avenue*. Beatrice became secretary of the new NAACP, organized in 1913 (the oldest continuously organized chapter west of the Mississippi) and fought discrimination and segregation in the community and the courts. In 1922, she became the first black woman to graduate from law school, attending night classes at the Northwest College of Law. Although she represented clients in court, she did not pass the Oregon Bar examination. After failing to be elected to the state legislature, she left Portland for good in 1936 and lived in California for the rest of her life.

35 THE GIPSY SMITH TABERNACLE

The Gipsy Smith Tabernacle, which stood on the northeast corner of *SW 12th Avenue and Morrison Street*, was named for a British evangelist and became a shelter for Portland's homeless in 1913. In that year, the Unemployed League drew nine thousand people to a rally in the Plaza Blocks demanding the city meet at least some of their desperate needs. As **Louise Bryant 30** wrote in *The Masses*, "men slept by the hundreds in the breezy tabernacle built for Gypsy [sic] Smith's revival meetings."[20] The men elected their own committee to run the "bunkhouse," including a barbershop and shoe repair, and negotiated with city and charity officials. By 1915, businessmen demanded the shelter close, saying: "it has become known throughout the Northwest that Portland has become a 'soft place' for the 'riffraff' of Seattle, Tacoma, and other Northwestern cities." Despite Edward Gilbert's declaration that the men of the Unemployed League wanted "work and not charity," the city closed the building a few months later. As Gilbert later told a public hearing, some food and shelter were provided, but he maintained, it wasn't a solution "to the unemployed problem."[21]

36 AGNES THECLA FAIR

On January 11, 1917, on the electric train tracks near SE Spokane Street in Sellwood, **Agnes Thecla Fair** committed suicide by throwing herself under a north-bound train. Fair, estimated to have been between thirty-five and forty-five years old when she died, was called a "dangerous character" by the Spokane police, who had molested her in jail during the IWW's Free Speech Fight in 1909. She raised money for the Wobblies by selling a volume of poems, *The Songs of Sourdoughs*, written during her years in Alaska, and in Spokane, Fair was arrested after wearing a "flaming red tie" while speaking to a large crowd. It was in jail where she declared herself an "author and playwright." She described that in her ordeal in the dark cell, she was surrounded by "ten big burley brutes." She wrote that she had "felt a large hand creeping over me." Unable to eat or sleep for the three days she was in jail, she was finally released and had to be taken out by her comrades on a stretcher. When Fair's account was published in Seattle's *Workingman's Paper* (Nov. 20, 1909), police tried to confiscate the entire edition for containing "indecent material."

Fair moved to Portland by 1911, when she introduced herself to **C. E. S. Wood 41** as a friend of **Emma Goldman 33**. She was an advocate for Albina's unemployed, and threatened to bring thirty children of unemployed fathers to City Hall—and for the hall to feed them when they got there—unless Mayor Rushlight provided work for the men. And later, as a public advocate for the starving, she demanded that Portland and Multnomah County hire hundreds for roadwork projects. She wrote several articles for *The Oregonian* on the success of women farmers, asserting that they did not need men to do the hard work. At the time of her suicide—reportedly because of "ill health"—she was staying at the Sellwood home of Mrs. Harriet Chervin, *487 Boundary Avenue.*

The Oregonian described her as a "sociological worker" and "well known in Portland as a woman of radical convictions, impetuous, ardent and active in her opposition to economic conditions which displeased her. She was an especial foe of the open shop [non-union employers]."

Her memorial service at the Finley Chapel was attended by "several score" of her Wobbly comrades led by her friend **Dr. Marie Equi 16**. Seattle Wobbly organizer Harry Lloyd was the main speaker at the service. Red carnations rested on her casket and "Workers of the World, Awake" and "The Red Flag" were sung in her honor.

The Red Flag

With head uncovered, swear we all,
To bear it onward till we fall;
Come dungeon dark or gallows grim,
This song shall be our parting hymn!

Agnes Thecla Fair's remains were escorted by a "cortege of comrades in belief" to the Portland Crematorium, where her ashes were held for the arrival of her divorced husband, W. P. Dougherty, from Coalinga, California.

37 PAPERMAKERS UNION STRIKE 1918

In 1917, Roy Ott and George Dunmire, who organized the **American Federation of Labor (AFL) Papermakers Union** at the Crown Willamette and Hawley Mills in suburban West Linn, were fired for union activities. Their fellow workers went on strike in protest. The mills were closed, but the owners brought in scabs (today, employers call them replacement workers), and the strike continued with widespread community support for over a year. Crown's manager B. F. McBain even built a hotel, The Swan, to house the non-union workers. It inspired "Hotel de Swan," an anonymous poem (credited to a six-year-old girl), which was published in the *Oregon City Morning Enterprise* on November 20, 1917:

> If McBain could break the unions here
> It would fill his heart with joy,
> He ne'er would hire those scabs again
> To work in his employ.
> He sets up good grub in the "Hotel de Swan"
> To keep their spirits gay
> But just the same the unions here
> Are on the strike to stay.

On June 23, 1918, a bloody confrontation between hundreds of scabs and strikers took place at the Oregon City end of the suspension bridge at *7th and Main Streets*. Kelley Loe of the *Oregon Labor Press* witnessed the battle, at which the local police, reportedly sympathetic to the strikers, were conspicuously absent. The strikers declared victory, but local business leaders demanded a coat of tar and feather for the union heads and the state Federation of Labor, who they called "Bolsheviki and riffraff." Eventually, the strike was broken and the mills were not unionized again until 1937. The "Hotel de Swan" became the West Linn Inn until it was demolished in 1985. The last mill in Oregon City closed in 1996.

38 HAZEL HALL 🌳

Poet **Hazel Hall** (1886–1924) was confined to a wheelchair for most of her short life and worked from the top floor of her family's house at 106 *NW 22nd Place*, where the Oregon Cultural Heritage Commission has placed a memorial. She is also honored on the sidewalk at TriMet's PGE Park MAX stop.

Hall published some of her work in the New York radical journal, *The Masses*, where **John Reed** 31 was an editor. The journal also published Portlanders **C. E. S. Wood** 41 and **Louise Bryant** 30. This poem, reminding us she was a seamstress, appeared in *The Masses* in 1917:

Needle, running in and out,
In and out, in and out,
Do you know what you're about,
In and out, in and out?
Fingers, going to and fro,
To and fro, to and fro,
Do you know the path you go,
To and fro, to and fro?
I might tell you why you're taking
Such good stitches: You are making
Out of linen fine as breaking
Ocean-spray upon a bluff,
Pleating for a Bishop's cuff!
I might make you understand
That a Bishop's white, white hand,
Because of you, will be more fair,
Will be raised in better prayer.
Even then you, would you know
Why you're going to and fro?
Would you doubt what you're about,
Running in and running out?

CHAPTER TWO:
Wobblies & Socialists

Colonel C. E. S. Wood supported local radicals like Emma Goldman, Margaret Sanger, and Dr. Marie D. Equi. He also served as a mentor to John Reed. *Oregon Historical Society, OrHi23607.* Inset: Colonel C. E. S. Wood as depicted on the front cover by Icky A. *Icky A.*

39 WESLEY EVEREST & THE CENTRALIA MASSACRE

Wesley Everest (1890–1919), the Wobbly and World War I veteran who was infamously lynched in the **Centralia Massacre** on Armistice Day 1919, was born in Newberg and grew up on his aunt's Westfall dairy near Portland. In 1914, he was captured in Coos County by a three hundred-strong vigilante gang of local businessmen and run out of town with other labor organizers. His grave in the Sticklin-Greenwood Memorial Park Cemetery in Centralia, Washington, was unmarked until the late 1930s. Old-timers located it in the southwest corner and the IWW erected a headstone.

40 OREGON SOCIALIST PARTY

In 1919, the **Oregon Socialist Party** was led by Harlin Talbert with offices at 529 SW 2nd Avenue, where he edited the *Oregon Socialist Party Bulletin.* In Portland the party had seven locals, which comprised over half of its two thousand members in the state. The largest was its West Side or "American" Local with 427 members, followed by the Scandinavian (300), Finnish (141), East Side "American" (101), German (75), Lettish (37), and Estonian (30).

41 COLONEL C. E. S. WOOD 🌐

Colonel C. E. S. Wood (1852–1944) was a military officer and radical lawyer who defended, among others, **Dr. Marie D. Equi 16**. He was also a dominant figure in Portland's civic and cultural life at the turn of the century until he moved to California in 1919. He supported local radicals like Equi, visitors like **Emma Goldman 33** and Margaret Sanger, and mentored others like **John Reed 31**. A friend of the dispossessed Chief Joseph of the Nez Perce, he sent his son Erskine Wood to spend summers with the Chief. All that remains of Wood's Portland home is the low brick balustrade along the patio of the Portland Garden Club at *1132 SW Vista Avenue*. His son's house, the Erskine Wood House, is at *2229 SW King Court*.

42 LOUISE HUNT 🌐

During World War I, **Louise Hunt** (1876–1960) was the assistant to Miss Mary Frances Isom, the Portland Library's head librarian, when the library had recently moved into a new building on *SW 10th Avenue*.[22] A committed pacifist at a time when a Methodist minister was urging the Portland Rotarians "if you have a pacifist, shoot him," she became a victim of Portland's World War I Red Scare in 1918 for refusing to buy war bonds. Although initially supported by the Library Board, its members caved before a flood of criticism from Portland power brokers and effectively fired her. The witch hunt against Portlanders accused of having a lack of enthusiasm for the war also cost Nell Moran, a Portland school teacher, her job and put **Dr. Marie Equi 16**, Henry Albers of Albers Milling Company, and Floyd Ramp of Eugene in jail.

43 THE COUNCIL OF WORKERS, SOLDIERS, AND SAILORS 🌐

The Council of Workers, Soldiers, and Sailors of Portland, which was inspired by the Soviets ("councils" in Russian) of the Russian Revolution, was organized by local radicals in January 1919 at Arion Hall. This building stood at *SW Oak Street and 2nd Avenue* until it was replaced by Portland Police Bureau Headquarters, and eventually became an office building.

The Council's organizer was Harry M. Wicks (1889–1956), the editor of the *Western Socialist* who had run for Congress on the Socialist Party ticket in 1918. The Council was organized to bring newly discharged servicemen together with unions in a new radical political movement. One of the Council's actions was to organize six hundred men in the Plaza Blocks to protest **Dr. Marie D. Equi's 16** sentencing to prison in 1918.

Replaced as council president by a foundry workers' union member, Wicks left the Council, and it dissolved after about six months. Wicks later became a Communist Party leader in the east and accompanied James W. Ford, the Party's black vice-presidential candidate, to Portland in 1932.

44 THE PORTLAND LABOR COLLEGE 🎤

The Portland Labor College, sponsored by the Central Labor Council and located in the Labor Temple at *SW 4th and Jefferson Street*, existed from 1921 to 1927,[23] and was briefly revived in the 1970s (see **Portland Labor College, Labor Education 169**). Its early life reflected tension between the radicals drawn to it and its sponsorship by the more conservative AFL craft unions. Its main organizer was Joseph Schwartrauler, head of the history department and the Portland Teachers Union at Lincoln High School. Its teachers included many Reed College faculty including Charles McKinley (later president of the American Political Science Association), E. O. Sisson, V. O. Chittick, William Griffith, G. B. Noble, and President Richard F. Scholz. They were joined by craftsmen such as radical Ray Neufer of the carpenters union and Works Progress Administration's (WPA) furniture designer fame. The late Aaron Director, a student of Schwartrauler who, after graduating from Yale, became Labor College director in 1924, invited **Elizabeth Gurley Flynn 53**, Scott Nearing, and other radicals to lecture at its forum. This soured his relations with the Central Labor Council and he left

This poster advertises a series of lectures at the Portland Labor College, *A Series of Six Lectures on Unemployment*, by Walter Thomas Mills. *Norm Diamond.*

Portland for a long and increasingly conservative career as an econo-mist at the University of Chicago. There he studied with future Illinois Senator Paul Douglas, who taught at Reed from 1916 to 1917. Director invited his sister Rose, who attended Reed, to become a graduate student in economics at the University of Chicago, where she met and married the future Nobel Prize winner Milton Friedman. In 1922, at the initia-tive of the Portland Teachers Union, the Labor College established the Portland Labor Players, the first and only workers' theater in the nation. The Players were under the direction of Doris Smith.

45 THE HOMEMADE PORTLAND REVOLUTION

Hoping for a general strike called **The Homemade Portland Revolution**, Portland Wobblies led a longshoremen strike in 1922 that was expanded to streetcar conductors. The strike incurred the wrath of the reaction-ary Mayor George L. Baker (1917–1933), a violent enemy of unions who had directed police raids against radicals during the first Red Scare several years earlier. Backed by the influential Ku Klux Klan of Portland and most businessmen, Baker threw four hundred strikers into Rocky Butte Jail. One of them, "Dublin Dan" Liston, used the time to write "The Portland Revolution," a song reprinted ever since in the IWW's *Little Red Songbook*. Its first verse goes:

> The Revolution started, so the Judge informed the Mayor,
> Now Baker paces back and forth, and raves and pulls his hair,
> The waterfront is tied up tight, the Portland newsboy howls,
> And not a thing is moving, only Mayor Baker's bowels.

46 FRANK T. JOHNS 🎤

Portland's only presidential candidate, **Frank T. Johns**, was the nominee of the SLP in 1924 and 1928. He was a member of Carpenters Union Local 226, which merged into today's Local 247, at *2215 NE Lombard Street*. Johns received about one thousand votes in Oregon and thirty-six thousand nation-wide in 1924, but on May 20, 1928, only weeks after his nomination, he died after a campaign speech on the banks of the Deschutes River in Bend. As the private memorial erected in 1970 relates, Johns dived into the river in a vain attempt to save two drown-ing boys but also drowned in the effort. His Portland Carpenters' Union

Frank T. Johns was the only presidential candidate to come from Portland. After giving a campaign speech in Bend, Oregon, Johns dived into the Deschutes River to save two boys from drowning. He died in the attempt. This memorial was erected in 1970. *Michael Munk.*

Local declared that their brother "had devoted his life to the working class" and died a hero, but they noted that the majority of his union's members "did not agree with his political theories."

47 PACIFIC COAST WORKERS SUMMER SCHOOL

In 1928, four students from Portland (and another eight from Astoria, Eugene, Clatskanie, Knappa, Marshfield, and Hood River) graduated from the **Communist Party's Pacific Coast Workers Summer School** in nearby Woodland, Washington. Portlanders Helen Harila, Eva Yank, and Alma Reinis were among the students at the school that summer who infiltrated a National Guard dance in Vancouver, Washington, to distribute anti-militarist pamphlets to their dancing partners. Henry Routu was the other Portland graduate.

1900–1930 NOTES

1. For more information about current the Socialist Party's Multnomah County Local meeting times visit: http://www.thesocialistparty.org/spo/pdx.

2. John Terry, *The Oregonian*, November 20, 2005.

3. Andrew Nils Bryans, "The Response to Left-Wing Radicalism in Portland, Oregon, from 1917 to 1941," (Unpublished MA Thesis, Portland State University, 2002).

4. William Z. Foster, *From Bryan to Stalin* (New York: International Publishers, 1937) 27.

5. William Z. Foster, *From Bryan to Stalin* (New York: International Publishers, 1937); E.P. Johanningsmeier, *Forging American Communism: The Life of William Z. Foster* (Princeton: Princeton University Press, 1994).

6. *The Oregonian*, March 25, 1905.

7. Tim Hills, "Myths and Anarchists: Sorting Out the History of Portland's White Eagle Saloon," *Oregon Historical Quarterly*, Winter 2000.

8. During the World War I period, about twenty states, including Oregon, passed laws making it a crime to defend, advocate, or set up an organization committed to the use of crime, violence, sabotage, or other unlawful means to bring about a change in the form of government or in industrial ownership or control.

9. K. W. Oster, "The Class War in Oregon," *The Toiler* (Cleveland) May 7, 1920.

10. *Don't Mourn—Organize: Songs of Labor Organizer Joe Hill*, Smithsonian Folkways CD 40026.

11. Lowell S. Hawley and Ralph Busnell Potts, *Counsel For the Damned: A Biography of George Francis Vanderveer* (J. B. Lippincott Co; 1st ed edition, 1953), esp. p 237–8, 271–2, 297–8.

12. Robert Hamburger, *Two Rooms: The Life of Charles Erskine Scott Wood* (Lincoln, NE: University of Nebraska Press, 1998).

13. See Martha Geis at the Eliot neighborhood website: http://eliotneighborhood.org/2009/07/21/historic-elks-lodge-grateful-for-volunteers.

14. Robert D. Johnston, "The Myth of the Harmonious City: Will Daly, Lora Little and the Hidden Face of Progressive-Era Portland," *Oregon Historical Quarterly*, Fall 1998.

15. Dorothy Reeves Wiley and Grace De Graff, undated typescript. Author's collection.

16. Michael Munk, "The Portland Years of John Reed and Louise Bryant" (Portland, OR: Oregon Cultural Heritage Commission, 3rd edition, 2003).

17. Michael Munk, "The 'Portland Period' of Artist Carl Walters," *Oregon Historical Quarterly*, Summer 2000; Munk, "The Diaries of Helen Lawrence Walters," *Oregon Historical Quarterly*, Winter 2005.

18. Kimberly Mangun, "As Citizens of Portland, We Must Protest: Beatrice Morrow Cannady and the African-American Response to D.W. Griffith's 'Masterpiece,'" *Oregon Historical Quarterly*, Fall 2006.

19. "Lifelong activist ready to talk race," *The Oregonian*, December 11, 1997.

20. "Two Judges," *The Masses*, April 1916.

CHAPTER TWO: Wobblies & Socialists

21. Dimitri Palmateer, "Charity and the 'Tramp': Itinerancy, Unemployment, and Municipal Government from Coxey to the Unemployed League," *Oregon Historical Quarterly*, Summer 2006.

22. Annette Bartholomae, "A Conscientious Objector: Oregon, 1918," *Oregon Historical Quarterly*, September 1970.

23. Jerry Lembcke, "Labor and Education: The Portland Labor College, 1921–1929," *Oregon Historical Quarterly*, Summer 1984.

Wobblies
& Socialists

To Seattle

V a n c o u v e r

63rd

I5

SR 500

1205

River Rd

4th Plain

E 5th

SR 14

C o l u m b i a

Bybee and Smith Lakes

Portland

Marine

R i v e r

Columbia Slough

W i l l a m e t t e   R i v e r

Columbia

Lombard

29

46

Greeley

Killingsworth

Hwy 30

MLK

Fremont

Sandy

Skyline

27

Rocky Butte

I84

Washington Park

Broadway

38

Cornell

13

29

To Coast

Burnside

Mt. Tabor Park

22

Lone Fir Cemetery

Sunset Hwy

28

Powell

Beaverton

52nd

33

Woodstock

Multnomah

36

Johnson Creek

Hwy 217

Macadam

30

I205

Tigard

Lake Oswego

McLoughlin

Lake Oswego

Tualatin River

5

I205

Miles

Wobblies & Socialists Downtown

Wobblies & Socialists Eastside

Wobblies & Socialists: Westside

CHAPTER THREE

UNIONS & COMMIES

1930s

Future Senator Richard Neuberger spoke to Reed College students at a 1938 peace rally on the Reed campus. He debated against war preparations, while his opponent, Oscar Gass, looked on.
Reed College Archives.

ortland joined in the surge of American radicalism during the
Great Depression of the 1930s. Its major expression was the
Communist Party, but the movement also included many other
Americans who had decided that laissez-faire capitalism was the cause
of intolerable human suffering and exploitation. The Communist Party's
work organizing much of the urban working class into the mass unions
of the new Congress of Industrial Organizations (CIO) was its major
achievement. This organizing was much more effective than its electoral politics, which mainly supported President Franklin Roosevelt
and his New Deal Democrats. In 1932, the Communists' leader, former
Portlander **William Z. Foster** 11, drew only 1,618 votes from Oregonians
in the Party's only presidential challenge of the decade.

Portland's most dramatic event of this period was its working class
participation in the great **West Coast Maritime Strike of 1934** 57, in which
thousands united to win union recognition and eventual control of
waterfront hiring. The victory came despite the city elite's hiring of
vigilantes, as well as **Bloody Wednesday at Terminal Four** 57 when police
shot and wounded striking longshoremen. The strike is still commemorated every July 5 in Oaks Park by area International Longshore and
Warehouse Union (ILWU) Locals, including Portland Local 8 and its
young Local 5, which represents workers at Powell's Books.

Both the ILWU and the former Portland-headquartered International
Woodworkers of America (IWA) were founded in the heyday of CIO
organizing, as was the **Oregon Workers Alliance (OWA)** 75. The OWA included
not only New Deal public works and construction workers, but also
radical artists and craftspeople supported by the federal Works Progress
Administration (WPA) such as the Runquist brothers and **Martina Gangle
Curl** 178. The painter Louis Bunce, whose once-controversial mural still
graces Portland International Airport, was secretary of the Oregon
office of the Federal Arts League. It was located in the same office in

the McKay Building that was previously occupied by the International Labor Defense (ILD). Bunce assisted on a WPA mural that can be seen at 8720 N. *Ivanhoe Street*. Formerly the St. Johns Post Office, it is now a Bahá'í Temple. Art community leaders who served on the Oregon committee included Reed professors Barry Cerf, V. L. O. Chittick, **Lloyd Reynolds** 128, and **Jessie M. Short** 85, as well as artists Virginia Darcey, **Dean William Givler** 131, and playwright **Dawn Lovelace** 64.

The Oregon Public Theater and art centers in Portland, La Grande (where **Minor White** 81 taught), Gold Beach, and Salem (where Bunce taught) provided both employment and cultural education to the Depression-era public. Many of Oregon's landmarks, such as Bonneville Dam (whose administrators hired **Woody Guthrie** 91 to write songs about it) and Timberline Lodge were built as part of the federal government's effort to provide jobs to the unemployed in the economic crisis, a response partly reflecting demands from the revived radical movement. WPA workers divided into five-man crews hauling carts and distributing ninety thousand black and white ceramic numbers that still mark many homes around the city. On the political front, the **Oregon Commonwealth Federation (OCF)** 76 offered a common home to radicals and liberals who shared the political goal of electing New Deal Democrats and defeating anti-Roosevelt conservatives in Oregon elections.

May Day became a major event for the Portland leftists in the 1930s. Formally known as "The International Day of the Working Class," it was originally observed locally by the Socialist Party. Before World War I and through the 1930s, events took place at today's **Lownsdale Square 9** (then called Plaza Park) at *SW Main Street between 3rd and 4th Avenues*.

May Day 1934 was especially dramatic; it dawned with a large red flag flying proudly over city hall. Demonstrators gathering at the nearby square were delighted that the flag remained most of the day due to a "malfunctioning" pole mechanism that defeated Mayor Joe Carson's efforts to remove it. The Portland section of the Communist Party proudly announced that the parade, which was dedicated against "hunger, fascism, and war," would use a "technological advance" — a public address system — for the first time in Portland. The Unemployed Councils, organized by the Communist Party, called on all working class organizations (and sympathizers) to march to Plaza Park to demand unemployment insurance and social security, free milk for children, "more and better relief," and the "release of all class war prisoners."

In 1938, the United Front May Day Committee organized a rally in the Civic Auditorium (now Keller Auditorium) to aid the Spanish Republic, which was then under fascist attack. Police **Red Squad 194** spies reported that this was "a complete change in tactics as experienced in former years when parades and soap boxing were the main events of May Day." Radicals returned to the Plaza Park Blocks for May Day 1939, when the Portland May Day Action Committee reminded the public that the tradition grew from an 1886 Chicago demonstration for the eight-hour day. The marchers called for labor unity, jobs, and social security, urging the public to back President Roosevelt.

Radicals were almost alone in organizing for civil rights for minorities and protesting racist court decisions, such as the **Theodore Jordan case 52** in 1932. In 1939, state Senator Herman Kenin of Portland introduced the first of what were later called "public accommodations" bills, prohibiting what was then routine racial discrimination in Oregon hotels, theaters, and restaurants. He was supported by testimony from **Irvin Goodman 71** on behalf of the International Labor Defense, Del Nickerson of the Oregon AFL, Edgar Williams of the Oregon NAACP, Catholic priest Walters of Astoria, Ms. Bowman of the Women's International League, and representatives of the Congregational Council for Social Action, the YWCA, the Portland High Schools Teachers Association, and several individuals.

After Oregon Apartment House Owners Association A. W. Orton shouted "Communism," and Earl McInnes of the Oregon Hotel Association declared that "hotels are the best friends the Negro people have," the bill was tabled by the Senate Judiciary Committee. A state public accommodations law was not passed until 1953.

CHAPTER THREE:
Unions & Commies

48 PAUL SIRO 🌐

Paul Siro (1911–1932) was dubbed "Astoria's Boy Communist" when, at fourteen, he was elected student body president at Robert Gray Junior High School and was quickly expelled for wearing a Lenin button to class. Siro was active in the Communist Party in Portland until May 1932, when he disappeared from his home at 785 N. *Minnesota Avenue* and was found dead in the Columbia River. His death remains a mystery and his headstone in Castle Rock's Hubbard-Whittle Cemetery reads: *Our Comrade.*

49 THE 1932 BONUS ARMY 🌐

In a movement that began in Portland, tens of thousands of World War I veterans joined **The Bonus Army** in 1932 to march on Washington, D.C., and demand expedited payment of promised bonuses. The Bonus Army began its march on Washington when three hundred men, led by former army sergeant and Burns-native Walter W. Waters (1898–1959), assembled at the Union Pacific railroad yards just north of the Broadway Bridge under a banner that read "Portland Bonus March — On to Washington." The vets, desperate because of the Depression, boarded a livestock train heading east. Waters was a superintendent at the Pacific Coast Fruit Company in Portland when the Depression cost him his job. At the Portland convention of the National Veterans Association that year, his proposal that "every man present hop freight and head for Washington to get the money that was rightfully theirs"[1] was enthusiastically received.

This Bonus March flier exhorted veterans to "March to your National Capital to save your country from those who continue to pillage it and deny you your just demands under a new administration." *City of Portland Archives, A2001-074.b2.f9.*

Several months later, the veterans calling themselves The Bonus Expeditionary Force were on their way in cattle cars from Portland. As the news spread, contingents organized around the nation. Eventually as many as 25,000 veterans set up an encampment at a Washington "Hooverville," a tent and shack refuge duplicated in every American city (including Portland) during the Depression. They elected Waters their commander-in-chief and vowed to stay until Congress appropriated the bonus money. They were denounced as Reds and savagely attacked by U.S. Army troops under the

This August 1932 protest in Lownsdale Square was billed as an antiwar rally. There were also signs demanding veterans be paid their bonus and for the release of labor leader Tom Mooney.
City of Portland Archives, A2001-74.91.

command of General Douglas MacArthur and aides Majors Dwight D. Eisenhower and George Patton. The Army killed two vets, burned the tent city, and caused one hundred casualties. Perhaps inspired by fascist organizing, Waters threatened to lead a "khaki-shirt" movement but instead got a federal job in Washington and led no more protests. He returned to his native Northwest in the 1950s and died in Wenatchee in 1959.

50 BEN BOLOFF 🌐

Ben Boloff (1893–1932), a Russian-born Communist ditch digger, is buried in River View Cemetery, at *8421 SW Macadam Avenue*. He lies together with members of prominent Portland families, including the Corbetts, Failings, Dolphs, Couches, Skidmores, Terwilligers, Cornells, Pittocks, Scotts, Ladds, and Greens—among the families he hoped the working class would replace in power. Boloff was a victim of Oregon's infamous Criminal Syndicalism Act under which he was sentenced to ten years in prison in 1930. He contracted tuberculosis, which his lawyer, **Irvin Goodman 71**, attributed to medical neglect in the Oregon State Penitentiary. After two years of passionate pleas by his comrades, Boloff was released to the Multnomah County Poor Farm (now McMenamins Edgefield Manor at *2126 SW Halsey Street in Troutdale*), when he was near death. The Party's leaflet for his mass funeral in the summer of 1932 says his last words echoed those of Frank Little, a Wobbly organizer who was lynched in Montana: "Tell the workers I fought for my class."[2]

This flier announced the demonstration and mass funeral procession for Ben Boloff, who died from tuberculosis shortly after being released from prison. *City of Portland Archives, A2001-074.*

51 THE PORTLAND FORUM 🎤

The Portland Forum, established by Rabbi Stephen S. Wise and **Colonel C. E. S. Wood 41** in 1905, provided lively public discussion of controversial subjects, including birth control and labor unions, along with scientific and medical topics. *The Oregonian* described it as:

> Like Hyde Park in London, this gathering comprises an intellectual melting pot which with its hurly-burly juxtaposition of good,

> *bad and indifferent oratory reveal a vibrant cross section of view-*
> *points in all point of life as harbored by white collar business*
> *and office men, soft-shirted workers, grey-garbed professional*
> *men, ambitious politicians, fervid students — occasionally a*
> *housewife. Fully 99 per cent of the [450 member] Forum audi-*
> *ence is made up of men who class themselves as philosophers,*
> *patriots, nationalists, socialists, communists, technocrats and an*
> *occasional single taxer or non-partisanist.*

After the new Central Public Library opened on *SW 10th Avenue between Taylor and Yamhill Streets*, it served as the organization's home until the Forum's demise during World War II.

Both of its two founders left Portland around 1920. Shortly after Wood moved to California, Wise resigned from the Portland Housing Code Advisory Committee, charging that it was "a front for realtors and homebuilders." He left the city to head New York's Central Synagogue. **Tom Burns 70**, one of the Forum's original members, became its informal "dean" through the late 1930s. In 1933, its permanent governing board included several members the **Red Squad 194** identified as Communists, including civil engineer Richard Lovelace and student Kenneth Fitzgerald.

52 THEODORE "TED" JORDAN 🌐

Theodore "Ted" Jordan (1908–1969), a black railroad worker, was named Oregon's Scottsboro Case by the leftist ILD in 1932, when he was sentenced to death by hanging for killing a white man in the Klamath Falls railroad yards. Radicals mounted a successful campaign to save Jordan from execution, also led by **Irvin Goodman 71** and the ILD, despite a bitter dispute over defense strategy with the Portland chapter of the National Association for the Advancement of Colored People (NAACP). In language that evokes the tenor of the times, Jordan wrote the following to promote the play *Pigment* by Portland radical **Dawn Lovelace 64**, produced by the ILD and the Save Jordan Anti-Lynch Committee, before several hundred people at the **Italian Federation Hall 182** at *SW 4th Avenue and Madison Street*, on May Day 1934. *The Oregonian* thought it noteworthy that the play was "acted by Negroes and whites."

*It is not an amusement, unless you can be amused by the
sufferings, gropings, trusting and awakening of the 12 million
Negro people and their ancestors for generations back. It is
not entertainment — unless the outcries of the Negro masses
are entertaining. It is not tragedy — for there is nothing tragic
about the uniting of the Negro and white millions, as they
smash the barriers set up between them, and march, however
painfully, toward a common liberation. It is drama — as
only workers can feel it and express it. I urge every Negro
worker — every white worker — to see it.*
— Theodore Jordan, *Death Cell, Oregon Penitentiary*

Governor Julius L. Meier, citing racial prejudice, commuted his death sentence to life imprisonment in 1934, but Jordan served another twenty years in the penitentiary, where he took courses through the University of Oregon's extension division. According to *The Oregonian*, he became "a leading figure in convict life." Following an alleged death-bed confession by another man to the murder, Jordan was finally paroled from the Oregon State Penitentiary in 1954. In 1961, he won a $500 settlement from Safeway for a false accusation of shoplifting, but he was convicted of a similar charge in 1963 and served another two years in prison when the courts ordered a new trial on the original murder charge. Ultimately, Klamath County declined to prosecute. Jordan took courses at Reed College and was working as a janitor in a downtown building, living quietly in a NE Garfield Avenue bungalow and writing an autobiography when he died of heart disease and diabetes at St. Vincent's Hospital in 1969.

Jordan's lighthearted, teasing death cell correspondence with Belle Taub, who was sent to Portland by the ILD from New York to help organize Jordan's defense, was stolen by the **Red Squad** 194 from ILD offices in room 307 of the McKay Building in a "black bag job." A sample reads:

*Just took a small work-out on the piano here and goodness
knows I am feeling like two million bucks even if it's in shekels
or kopecks. Some day I may whip up a few hot numbers for
you, provided you can stand it without calling the riot squad.
Even if I do say so myself, I seem to run Cab Calloway and*

Duke Ellington a very close second when it come to spanking the ivories, I plunk 'em mean or let 'em, alone — that's Mrs. George's [his mother's] boy as I live and breathe.

Only after Ted Jordan's death sentence for murder did the NAACP hire Portland attorney Charles W. Robison to file an appeal for a stay of execution and a new trial. But Jordan asked the leftist International Labor Defense, led in Oregon by attorney Irvin Goodman, and supported by future federal judge Gus Solomon, Goodman's partner Leo Levenson, and a "Mr. Seltzer" to represent him and generate public support. Robison immediately dropped out because the "NAACP can in no way be aligned with Communism." But he also went on to gratuitously denounce Jordan as "too smart for your own good and too ignorant for anyone else's good," and charged him of being "a curse and not a help to your own [black] people." Levenson was also one of several Portland attorneys to represent "unfriendly" witnesses before HUAC in 1954.

Levenson is honored by Lewis & Clark Law School, whose graduating classes annually award the Leo Levenson Award for Excellence in Teaching.

53 ELIZABETH GURLEY FLYNN

Elizabeth Gurley Flynn (1890–1964) lived with **Dr. Marie D. Equi** 16 at her home at 1433–39 SW Hall Street most of the time for ten years from the fall of 1926 until around 1936. Flynn was a leader in radical politics throughout her life. As a pregnant young Wobbly, she was jailed overnight in Spokane during the IWW's free speech fights in 1909; as a sixty-four-year-old leader of the Communist Party during the McCarthy Era, she was imprisoned from 1955 to 1957 under the Smith Act. Flynn fell ill with heart problems in San Francisco on a tour to support Nicola Sacco and Bartolomeo Vanzetti, Italian anarchists accused of a Boston-area bank robbery. Wobbly Joe Ettor drove her to Portland, where her closest friend, Equi, lived. Flynn was able to give her speech in Portland, Seattle, and Spokane, but then Equi insisted she return for medical care—advice which Flynn later credited with saving her life.

For the next decade, Flynn's life in Portland was withdrawn and sedentary for multiple reasons: her own poor health, depression after Sacco and Vanzetti were electrocuted in the fall of 1927, and the need to care for her housemate, Equi, who had also developed heart trouble. In 1929, her health had improved enough to permit her to speak in Portland for Tom Mooney and the Wobblies jailed after the **Centralia Massacre 39**. Despite Flynn and Equi's poor health, the **1934 Longshore Strike 57** energized them both. Flynn recalled her anger that "workers' blood was shed." She and Equi contributed a joint article on the first anniversary of Portland's **Bloody Wednesday 57** to the radical Seattle paper *Voice of Action*. In 1936, Flynn's sister Bina came to Portland and demanded that Flynn leave with her to New York. Flynn moved there in July of that year. [3]

Later, as a Communist Party leader, Flynn visited Portland often, writing her observations about the political consequences of the **Vanport Flood 115** and speaking at a 1943 May Day Victory Rally in **Redmen Hall 120**. Her first public lecture after her release from prison was in May 1958 at Reed College. She went to Moscow for medical treatment and died there in 1964. Some of her ashes were buried near **John Reed's 31**.

54 NEW GOLDEN WEST HOTEL 🍸

In the 1930s, *Harlemania*, a filmed musical review, played nightly at the **New Golden West Hotel** at *707 NW Everett Street*. The musical was also featured at a rally there for the Scottsboro Boys sponsored by the ILD.

The hotel was a center of black community life for the first half of the twentieth century, when it welcomed black railroad workers from nearby Union Station. From 1906 to 1931, it was managed by W. D. Allen. Mrs. Catherine Byrd took over the job in 1933. Over the years, it housed Richard Waldo Bogle's barber shop, a Chinese restaurant, a saloon, an ice cream parlor, a candy store, and a speakeasy during Prohibition — old timers recall having their first drinks there, when a whiskey sour was a quarter. [4]

In 2009, the hotel's place in Portland's black community was recognized with sidewalk exhibits showing and narrating its history.

55 KARL MARX SALTVEIT 🍸

Karl Marx Saltveit (1906–1978) was named in honor of the German philosopher and economist by his Norwegian Communist father. He anglicized his name to "Carl" and put it on his barbershop at *2946 NE Glisan Street* in the early 1930s. In 2006, the site was occupied by what claimed to be Portland's oldest body-piercing salon. Saltveit named his own son, a former Oregon Deputy Labor Commissioner, Carl Marcus, who in turn, named the family's next first-born male Carl Mark.

The black-owned Golden West Hotel catered to railroad workers. Its theater showed *Harlemmania* in the 1930s. *Oregon Historical Society, OrHi12187.*

The Carl Marx Barber Shop was located at 2946 NE Glisan Street in the early 1930s. *Carl Saltveit.*

56 KIRK'S DONUT SHOP 🌐

Where the Union Gospel Mission now stands on the northwest corner of *W. Burnside and NW Third Avenue* was the site of **Kirk's Donut Shop** in the 1930s. Kirk's was a hangout for radicals during the **1934 longshore strike 57**, as depicted in a painting by radical artist Pele deLappe (1916–2007).[5] DeLappe had come to Portland from San Francisco to be with her lover Sam Telford, organizer of the Marine Workers Industrial Union at nearby *217 NW Davis*. DeLappe identified the people in her painting as: MWIU leader Hays Jones, **Dirk DeJonge 63**, Hal Spring, and Bay-area radicals Henry Glixon (a Communist Party organizer, AKA Harry Jackson) and International Labor Defense leader Elaine Black Yolanda as the waitress. DeLappe recalled being "fed up with Portland's constant grey wetness" but still "mounted soapboxes on Skid Row (*sic*) exhorting winos to join the union [and making] posters for mass meetings." After returning to San Francisco, she produced this "remembered scene [at Kirk's] on a cold rainy night seen through a steamy window, peopled with some of my comrades." In later life, deLappe's close companion was the "Oregon Hillbilly" artist Byron Randall — originally from Salem.

57 1934 MARITIME STRIKE & THE INTERNATIONAL LONGSHORE AND WAREHOUSE UNION (ILWU) 🌐

The outstanding Portland event of the 1930s was the **Maritime Strike of 1934**. The event climaxed when police shot and wounded four striking longshoremen at St. Johns Terminal Four at *11040 N. Lombard Street* on July 11, the day referred to as Bloody Wednesday. While not as notorious as San Francisco's Bloody Thursday of July 5, 1934, when police killed two workers, it was seen as a major battle of Portland's class war. The shooting was instigated by Mayor Joe Carson, who had tried to break the strike by escorting scabs through picket lines and deputizing Citizens Emergency Committee vigilantes as special police. But on Bloody Wednesday he ordered regular Portland police to escort a train onto the struck docks. The police fired on the picket line assembled on the railroad tracks in Pier Park wounding Burt Yates, E. W. Beatty, W. Huntington, and Peter Stevenson.

At city hall, strike leader Matt Meehan confronted the mayor with the blood-soaked shirt of one of the wounded and yelled: "You're responsible for this!" After this incident the mayor was forever known in the labor community as Bloody Shirt Carson.

The Oregon National Guard was called in to man the barricade against strikers at the Multnomah County Armory at NW 10th Avenue and Couch Street. *Oregon Historical Society, CN005984.*

Portland Police escorted "scabs" through picket lines outside a hiring hall, a building used by companies to hire workers. *Oregon Historical Society, OrHi81704.*

In August 1934, twenty-nine innocent ILA men were arrested and jailed for a month on homicide charges. Marvin Ricks (left), the last surviving Portland veteran of the 1934 Strike, was one of those innocent men. This pin (inset) was worn by their supporters. *Michael Munk.*

A week later, President Roosevelt sent New York Senator Robert Wagner to Terminal Four to smooth the waters, but Wagner's party was also fired upon. Although the incident was presumed a mistake, this time the fault was in the hands of the special police. The strike ended in victory for the longshoremen a few days later and led to the formation of today's **ILWU**. Several Oregon communities are home to locals of this union, including Portland Locals 8 (longshore), 40 (checkers), 90 (walking bosses), 5 (Powell's Books), 28 (Kaiser Permanente security), 50 (Astoria), 12 (North Bend), and the Columbia River Pensioners Association. Every year since 1934, on Bloody Thursday the ILWU

Richard Correll's labor woodcuts began appearing in the Seattle paper *Voice of Action* in the 1930s. This one, titled *Bloody Wednesday at Terminal 4* appeared on the one-year anniversary of that date in 1935. *Michael Munk.*

commemorates the strike in every port on the Pacific Coast. For much of that time, Portland longshoremen marched through downtown to the sea wall, but now they meet at Oaks Park. According to veterans of the 1934 strike, Portlanders could still dig police bullets out of the big firs at Pier Park many years later.

58 ALBINA HALL 🎙

On August 20, 1934, **Albina Hall** at *1401 NE Alberta Street* was the scene of a violent shootout in one of the last bloody consequences of the great **1934 Maritime Strike 57**. The hall was still being used to dispatch scabs belonging to a company "blue book" union controlled by the waterfront employers, although the strike had officially ended in a famous union victory several weeks earlier. Longshoremen demonstrated outside the hall against the scabs and one of them, James Connor, was shot and killed inside the hall. Police arrested twenty-nine ILA members on homicide charges and jailed them for about a month before the charges were dropped. The twenty-nine innocent men included former Wobbly and radical strike leader William Pilcher,[6] as well as retired longshoreman Marvin Ricks, the last surviving Portland veteran of the 1934 strike. Ricks says Connor was probably shot accidentally by his fellow scabs, who, led by the notorious **Red Squad 194** provocateur Harper Knowles, fired at the union demonstrators from inside the hall.

59 THE MARINE WORKERS INDUSTRIAL UNION 🌐

During the 1934 **Maritime Strike 57**, **The Marine Workers Industrial Union**, a Communist-backed radical alternative to the American Federation of Labor's (AFL) corrupt ILA, had its headquarters in the Musolf Manor Building (the former Foster Hotel) at *217 NW Davis Street*. Portland police raided it twice in July 1934, and its leaders were charged with violating the Oregon Criminal Syndicalism Act.

Nearby at *9 NW 3rd Avenue*, five women strike sympathizers working at the Villa Rooms—Margie, Kay, Florence, Helen, and "Smiles"—prepared sandwiches for the strikers (delivered by Broadway Cab drivers to the picket lines for free) and signed a card for them. It was rumored that they also provided strikers with other services on credit for the duration of the strike.

The 1934 strike veteran who provided this card says "Smiles" was the working name of one of the five women. To the end of his 94-year life, he always took a Broadway Cab because their drivers delivered those sandwiches to the picket lines for free.

60 *ADMIRAL EVANS* 🌐

A major event in the **1934 Maritime Strike 57** was the strikers' attack on the ***Admiral Evans***, a scab hotel tied up at McCormick Dock just north of the Steel Bridge. Strikebreakers hired by the Citizens Emergency Committee were brought into Portland and housed aboard the ship. On May 11, as many as one hundred longshoremen formed what they called a riot squad, and, after attacking armed guards, the group succeeded in boarding the vessel. The pitched battle ended with injured on both sides, but the longshoremen were victorious. Many of the special police had to swim for safety in the Willamette River, as the *Admiral Evans* drifted downstream until it wedged against the Broadway Bridge.

61 THE UNION HALL 🌐

During the 1934 strike, the ILA **Union Hall** was at *NW Everett Street between 8th and 9th Avenues*. Across the street was the former French's Restaurant, where the strikers used the phone to coordinate resistance

The Union Hall was once located in what is now McMenamins Mission Theater at NW 16th Avenue and Glisan Street. *Colin Smith.*

by tracking scab movements with roving "riot" and picket squads. When longshoremen voted to organize the CIO's ILWU in 1937, they retained the old building as their hiring hall. After some years at *1624 NW Glisan Street* (now McMenamins Mission Theater), Local 8 built a new hall at *2435 NW Front Street*, near the former Molly McGuires tavern, which was named after the militant nineteenth century Irish miners' union in the Pennsylvania coal fields, until it later burned down.

62 LIEUTENANT WILLIAM EPPS 🌐

Portland Police **Lieutenant William Epps** suffered a black eye on the second day of the 1934 Maritime Strike, when strikers prevented scabs from being bussed from the Everett Street hall. But Lt. Epps, a former organizer of the mineworkers' union, was evidently a working-class sympathizer. In 1932, he dissuaded his superiors from ordering an attack on an unemployed demonstration at the Benson Hotel at *309 SW Broadway.* Rumor has it that later in the 1934 strike, Epps tipped off the strikers about when and where police were escorting scabs.

Epps's son, David C. Epps, was a member of the **OCF 76**, and **American Friends of China 74** in the late 1930s.

63 DIRK DEJONGE 🌐

Communist leader **Dirk DeJonge** (1891–1976) was imprisoned for almost two years, under Oregon's Criminal Syndicalism Act, for chairing a meeting to protest vigilante violence during the **1934 Maritime Strike 57**. In 1935, the ILD produced a play, *The Trial of Dirk DeJonge*, at the Woodmen of the World Hall at *SW 11th Avenue and Alder Street*. This play was part of a program in which *Art Dancing* by attorney Nick Chaivoe was featured. DeJonge remains prominent in legal history in the case *DeJonge vs. Oregon*, where the U.S. Supreme Court ruled the Oregon law could not be used to convict a person for speech alone. DeJonge's "intended wife," Ella Badgley, wrote poignant but unsuccessful letters pleading his good character to the sentencing judge, Judge Jacob Kanzler, from her home at *23 N. Graham Street*. The letters found their way to the **Red Squad 194** and can be consulted in its files in the city archives.

Communist leader Dirk DeJonge was imprisoned for nearly two years for chairing a meeting protesting vigilante violence during the 1934 strike. His mug shot was taken on July 18, 1934.
City of Portland Archives, A2001-74.

64 MAJOR LAWRENCE A. MILNER & DAWN LOVELACE 🌐

During the DeJonge trial at the Multnomah County Court House at *1021 SW 4th Avenue*, **Major Lawrence A. Milner** won applause from radicals when he revealed that special Oregon state prosecutor Stanley Doyle visited him at his home and offered to exchange his testimony against DeJonge for help on his government pension. However, Milner's declaration was an act to conceal that since 1933, he was a full-time paid undercover agent for Governor Charles "Iron Pants" Martin's National Guard.[7] While pretending to work for Left organizations through 1937, he wrote daily reports on leftist activities that today total about 1,400 in the State Archives in Salem. When he came out as a witness against longshore union leader Harry Bridges in his deportation hearings, the deportation hearings chair recommended Milner "best be dismissed as a self-confessed liar."

Doyle was a notorious political extremist sponsored by the Commanders Council, which was comprised of leaders of the American Legion and other right-wing and veterans groups. Portland radical **Dawn Lovelace** attacked him in her poem, *Stanley Doyle — Voice of Hunger, War and Fascism*, a stanza of which reads:

> He sneers — and from his mouth
> The Reichstag flames leap menacing and hot;
> And all the outcries of the tortured minds and bodies
> In fascist dungeons spring to vivid sound
> And echo in the courtroom

65 THELMA JOHNSON STREAT 🌳

Thelma Johnson Streat (1911–1959) was a black artist who grew up in Portland and graduated from Washington High School in 1932. She lived at *1409 SE Lambert Street* from 1934 to 1935 while she attended the Museum Art School on a scholarship from **Paul Robeson 136**. She then moved to San Francisco to work as a WPA artist. The radical Mexican muralist Diego Rivera, who owned some of Streat's work, considered it "one of the most interesting manifestations of American art…extremely evolved and sophisticated enough to reconquer the grace and purity of African and American art." Her paintings were also purchased by the Museum of Modern Art in New York City, and by Hollywood celebrities. Although she left Portland for California in 1936, Streat later made visits to Portland as a dancer. Reed College holds her painting, *Black Virgin*, in its permanent collection. Pacific Northwest College of Art (successor to the Museum Art School) honored Streat by awarding her (to her family) a Doctor of Arts degree honoris causa at its 2010 Commencement Ceremony.

66 AMY (OMA) WOODCOCK SINGER 🔌

As a Chinook Indian and the first and only Native American student at Reed College in the 1930s, **Amy (Oma) Woodcock Singer** (1916–) participated in Portland **protests against fascist ships 74** and supported the **1934 longshore strikes 57**. She was also a member of Virginia Darcy's Skidmore Artists Association, according to Murphy's book (see below). A retired social worker, Singer lives at *5535 East Evergreen Boulevard* in Vancouver. Singer turned down Communist Party membership because she feared the Department of Interior would revoke her Indian Bureau scholarship, but she still remained active in the party. The atmosphere of Portland radicals in those years was closely chronicled by her classmate Doris Bailey Murphy in the opening chapters of her autobiographical book *Love and Labor* (iUniverse, 2006). Amy Singer was a babysitter for the author in 1939.

67 BEN BARZMAN 🔌

During the 1930s, the building at *707-15 NE Broadway* was the garment factory Beaver Suit and Cloak. According to his widow Norma Barzman, that was where **Ben Barzman**, later a blacklisted Hollywood screen writer, "stood on his feet for ten years while putting himself through Reed College."[8] His thesis there was "The Wind is Our Heritage: A Three-Act Play." He went on to Los Angeles, where he wrote scripts for films such as *El Cid, The Blue Max,* and *The Boy with Green Hair.* As were most leftists who refused to inform on their colleagues, Ben and Norma were blacklisted in Hollywood in 1949, and went into exile in Europe. There, Ben wrote *The Visit* and Z, and they did not return to the U.S. until 1976.

In 1999, his credits for El Cid were posthumously restored by the Writers Guild of America. Barzman also contributed the brilliant essay "A Small Vineyard" to a *festschrift* published by Reed College honoring Professor **Lloyd Reynolds 128**, one of Reed's victims of McCarthyism.

68 MARK ROTHKO 🔌

The prominent artist **Mark Rothko** (1903–1970) arrived in Portland as Marcus Rothkowitz from Russia at the age of ten and lived first at *3434 SW Front Street.* After graduating from Lincoln High School in 1921, both he and his friend Aaron Director received scholarships to Yale. Both were interested in Socialism and wanted to become labor union organizers. Like his father, Rothko believed strongly in workers' and women's rights. At Yale, the two Portlanders started a magazine called *The Yale Saturday Evening Pest*, which made fun of the school's "stuffy, and bourgeois" attitude and described Yale culture as "elitist and racist." After his second year (which he paid for himself), Rothko dropped out and didn't return until Yale awarded him an honorary degree in 1968.

Rothko and his wife visited Portland in 1933, and camped in Washington Park, where they were cited by police for "public nudity."

Rothko's first Portland home was in a duplex at *3434 SW Front Avenue*. The west side of the Front Avenue block between SW Curry and SW Whittaker was destroyed by the widening of Front Avenue (today's SW Naito Parkway) after World War II. The building in Rothko's unnamed, late 1920s sketch is of the view from his later home on SW Lincoln Street, now an office building on SW Terwilliger Boulevard.

69 DR. DENORVAL UNTHANK 🌐

The prominent black physician **Dr. DeNorval Unthank** was a special target of **Major Lawrence A. Milner 64**. When Unthank arrived in Portland in 1930 to practice medicine, he and his wife were forced to move five times for reasons that included being harassed from the Ladd's Addition neighborhood. On August 20, 1935, Milner accompanied Esther Murphy, wife of Communist leader James Murphy, to meet Unthank in his offices at *SW 6th Avenue and Burnside Street* to discuss a meeting on the Italian invasion of Ethiopia to be held at what was then called the Colored Elks Temple. Unthank offered to contact black churches and the YMCA to promote the meeting and said his wife had just returned from Ethiopia and would speak. Milner's report to the Oregon National Guard concludes: "Unthank is a party sympathizer, as he has various literature in his office and from his statements he is very anxious to promote any work that is sponsored by the party." A few days later, Milner observed Ken Fitzgerald, a Portland reporter for the Seattle labor paper, *Voice of Action*, interview Unthank about the racist obstacles he faced practicing his profession in Portland.

Unthank's son, DeNorval Jr., an architectural student at the University of Oregon, met student Debbie Burgess in the spring of 1951. They soon called themselves the "salt and pepper" couple and encountered the full force of Oregon racism on the Eugene campus. The sisters of Debbie's sorority asked her to leave the house, and when she didn't comply quickly enough, a 7-foot Ku Klux Klan cross was burned on the Gamma Phi Beta lawn. The Oregon legislature had just repealed the state's 1866 ban on

Dr. DeNorval Unthank is the only "Communist Party sympathizer" to have a Portland park named for him. Unthank Park is located on N. Commercial Avenue. *Oregon Historical Society, OrHi25442.*

interracial marriage, in May, 1951. The vote in the Senate was 21–7, in which three Portland-area Senators voted to keep the ban—Thomas Mahoney (the only Democrat among the seven), Frank Hilton, and Eugene Marsh (Yamhill). But the couple felt more secure going across the river to an Episcopalian church in Vancouver to marry. The fact that the groom's father was a prominent Portlander doesn't completely explain why *The Oregonian* reported his son's marriage to a white woman on its front page, or why a story in *Time Magazine* was warranted.

The marriage produced three children until they divorced in 1972. DeNorval became a successful architect, and died in 2000 at the age of 71. The couple's courage in breaking the marriage color line was celebrated by *Oregonian* columnist Steve Duin.

The only Portland park named for a "Communist Party sympathizer" is Unthank Park on *N. Commercial Avenue between N. Failing and Shaver Streets.* In 2010, a local gang took the name, "Unthank Park Hustlers."

70 TOM BURNS 🍎

Tom Burns's (1876–1957) famous Clock Shop was located at 221 W.

Burnside Street for many years until his death. The son of a British Labor Party member of Parliament, Burns arrived in Portland from Liverpool in 1905. In Portland, he originally joined the Socialist Party but soon found the IWW more congenial and opened his shop as The Bookery at *22 SW 4th Avenue*, and later opened the Clock Shop, a clock and watch repair shop on Burnside with a radical lending library in the basement. He published *FAX*, an irreverent newsletter that attacked the Right as well as his opponents on the Left, like the Communist Party. He was known both as "the mayor of Burnside" and "the most arrested man in Portland's history."[9]

Stewart Holbrook recalled meeting many famous radicals in the Clock Shop's "stygian" basement. Among them were "Big Jim Thompson, the Wobbly speaker, Elmer Smith, the young IWW attorney [who defended the **Centralia Wobblies 39**] **Arthur 'Old War Horse' Boose 90**, a hero of the Mesabi Strike in Minnesota, Mrs. Tom Mooney, Harry Kemp, the tramping-on-life poet, and various speakers-up for plain socialism, Laborite-Socialism, for both the Orthodox and Emergency Program [factions] of the Industrial Workers of the World." Holbrook also revealed that Burns kept in his window a large gas cigar lighter called "Lady Luck," which he got from Erickson's Saloon down the block. Lady Luck was a cast metal head and bust of a "charming female from whose pretty mouth protruded a round pipe, of cigarette size and shape, from which a tiny flame of gas issued, year upon year, for the convenience of the patrons." When Burns died, Holbrook was happy that Lady Luck "had the great good fortune to fall into the loving hands of **Francis J. Murnane 171**, of the **International Longshoremen 57**, whom I first met long ago in Tom's place. As a lad, Murnane used to admire [Lady Luck] when he'd sneak into Erickson's to see 'The Longest Bar in the World' and her who lighted the cigars of men who had hair on their chests and faces."[10]

During the 1930s, Burns frequently denounced "Portland's political parasites—the first families like the Corbetts, Labbes, Wilcoxes—coupon clipping clowns that never did a useful day's work in their worthless lives." Howard Morgan, a leader of the Oregon Democratic Party in the 1950s and 1960s, credits Burns as an important influence in his decision to enter politics.[11] The radical tradition of that Burnside intersection continued until just a few years ago. In 1996, the storefront next to Burns's former store was unwittingly occupied by an anarchist group, some of who had ties to a resurrected IWW organization, and in

Tom Burns's bookstore, the famous Clock Shop, was located at 22 SW 4th Avenue. Burns was a member of both the Socialist Party and then the IWW. He was known both as "the mayor of Burnside," and "the most arrested man in Portland's history." He had a radical lending library in the basement of Clock Shop and published *FAX*, an irreverent newsletter attacking both the Right and the Left. *Walt Curtis.*

The interior of Clock Shop. *Walt Curtis.*

2001, a neighboring building was the site of an anarchist "Center for Revolution." Until a few days before he died in 1957, Burns used streetcars or buses to get to his shop from his home at *5913 SE 49th Avenue,* just off Woodstock Boulevard, which is now a vacant lot.

71 IRVIN GOODMAN 🎙

Portland's most celebrated radical attorney, **Irvin Goodman** (1897–1958), rose to prominence in the 1930s. In 1940, he shared his office with Leo Levenson in suite 1002 of the Spaulding Building, having previously shared it with the future Federal Judge Gus Solomon. Goodman, a 1921 Reed College graduate, played a leading role in most of the important defenses of radicals and minorities in Portland throughout his professional life, including the famous *DeJonge vs. Oregon Supreme Court Decision* 63. Goodman was especially active in civil rights, defending such prominent victims of racism as **Theodore "Ted" Jordan** 52 and **Wardell Henderson** 113. Also among his clients were many victims of McCarthyism, including Soviet naval officer **Lt. Nicolai Redin** 100 and defiant witnesses at the 1954 **House Un-American Activities Committee (HUAC)** 128 hearings in Portland. Honored by the American Veterans Committee, the **Oregon Committee for Protection of the Foreign Born** 139, and the **ILWU** 57, he is buried in the Kesser Israel cemetery at *SE 67th Avenue and Nehalem Street.* Progressive law offices in Portland closed on his death, and Julia Ruuttila published this thought in the *People's World* (July 12, 1958) on his passing:

On the skidroads of the Northwest, under the tall firs, on the net racks of Greys [H]arbor, Astoria and Puget Sound, in the tenements where the old timers on social security remember the picket lines and bread lines of their youth, the workers who never forget observed their moments of silence for Irvin Goodman.

72 GRACE WICK

Grace Wick (1888–1958) was an activist and actress whose politics were a strange mixture of liberalism and far-right reaction. She moved to Portland from Salem in the mid-1920s after losing a struggle to prevent the hanging of Barney Cody, a cousin of Buffalo Bill, who was tried for murder. Originally a supporter of FDR, she managed to include herself in the president's party when he dedicated Bonneville Dam in 1934. She became disillusioned when the New Deal failed to end the Great Depression and turned her support to the Ku Klux Klan, America First, and anti-Semitic groups. Her famous march up Broadway in 1935 marked her break from the Left when one of the slogans on her barrel read "Wake Up Unemployed. Organize Now!" She ran for local and state office in the late 1930s and 1940s as a right-wing activist. Her future partner, Fred Melanson, wrote a campaign poem for her that included the line "To Oregon a Goddess came, who fights for the oppressed."[12]

Wick died in Portland in 1958.

73 BURL (B. A.) GREEN

The courageous Portland attorney **Burl (B. A.) Green** often represented labor unions, especially during the 1930s. He tried to organize an Oregon chapter of the **American Civil Liberties Union (ACLU) 123**, and chaired a December 1937 meeting at the Multnomah County Courthouse that exposed the illegal operation of the **Red Squad 194**. For his efforts, the Red Squad listed him as an "active Communist sympathizer." His record also includes defending Wobblies arrested in Tillamook while maintaining friendly personal relations with prominent Portlanders.

74 PROTESTING FASCISM

Portland radicals, led by the Communist Party, tried to warn Oregonians

Grace Wick, an activist and actress, had a strange mix of liberalism and far-right reaction in her politics. She's shown here, in 1935, during a political march in Portland. *Oregon Historical Society, CN023435.*

about the threat of fascism. One of their efforts was to protest the arrival of fascist ships, as in January 1936, when police arrested eleven Portlanders[13] demonstrating against the **Nazi cruiser** *Emden* docked at the foot of *SW Couch Street.* As *The Oregonian* described it, the *Emden's* symbol was "the 'new deal' flag of Germany, the swastika, emblem of Hitler, unfurled to the breezes of Portland." The ship's officers visited Mayor Joseph Carson in his office, where "they clicked their heels in military fashion and gave him the German [Heil Hitler] salute." Most German organizations in Portland arranged welcoming entertainment for the crew. Until 1936, the *Emden* was commanded by future Grand Admiral Karl Doenitz who, as Hitler's successor, formally surrendered Nazi Germany in 1945. In addition to the demonstration at the sea-wall, the Portland section of the Communist Party called on unions

The German ship Emden was enthusiastically welcomed by Portland's powerful in 1936. Radicals protested it. *Historical Photo Archive, Monner 2271.*

and Jewish organizations to send protest delegations to the mayor and urged maritime unions to strike when the *Emden* docked.

The previous October, during the fascist invasion of Ethiopia, the Communist Party organized a significant picket line at the Clark-Wilson and Oceanic Terminal to protest the docking of the Italian cargo ship the *S.S. Cellini,* asking longshoremen to "Load No Cargo for Fascist Italy" and to "Turn around Mussolini's Ship of Death." Also in 1935, the Portland branch of the American League Against War and Fascism picketed the office of Robert Clostermann, the German consul in the Stock Exchange Building, declaring, "We Want No Fascism Here!" In 1938, protests by the **American Friends of China** (which, ironically, had its office in room 507 of the same building), and **OWA 75,** supported by Willamette Lodge 63 of the International Association of Machinists, targeted the Japanese training ship *Taisei Maru.* This ship docked at the foot of SW Ankeny Street for several days, and was welcomed by the Chamber of Commerce. At least fifteen people, including **Martina Gangle Curl 178,** were arrested. Gus Karju, whose sailboat towed a float demanding "Stop Killing the Chinese" and "Japanese not welcome," was charged with "obstructing the river."

75 OREGON WORKERS ALLIANCE ♀

The 1936 Rose Festival parade featured an **OWA** float with **Martina Gangle Curl 178** as the Statue of Liberty. The association developed from

Portland's radicals protested the U.S. support of Japan in its war with China. The Women's Committee of the American League for Peace and Democracy is shown at the waterfront in 1937. *City of Portland Archives, A2001-074.23.*

the unemployed councils organized by the Oregon Communist Party early in the Great Depression. The councils demanded public relief and public works programs, and offered social activities such as the Hawthorne branch's "Chicken dinner, plenty of coffee, entertainment and dancing—all for 25 cents," at **Redmen Hall** 120, *1510 SE 9th Avenue* at Hawthorne Boulevard. After several mergers with similar groups, the OWA emerged and described itself in Wobbly terms as the one big union of the unemployed, part-time workers, and workers on WPA and other relief projects. In addition to its original goals, the OWA was active in supporting families who were rejected for public welfare and were resisting evictions and utility cutoffs. During the McCarthy Era, some of its foreign-born working class members were deported or threatened with deportation. The OWA was organized into neighborhood locals, such as Abernethy Local No. 23, which met in the Abernethy School auditorium, then at *SE 14th Avenue at Division*. Its state office was in the **Governor Building** 86 at *408 SW 2nd Avenue*.

76 OREGON COMMONWEALTH FEDERATION & MONROE SWEETLAND 🌐

The **OCF**, a liberal and radical coalition of New Deal supporters founded in 1936 with a local electoral agenda, had its offices in the Stock Exchange Building at *170 SW 3rd Avenue*. Under the leadership of **Monroe Sweetland** (1910–2006), who later became a prominent Democrat, the OCF backed several successful campaigns for the state

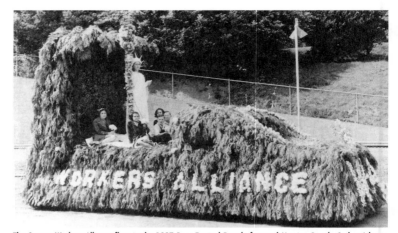

The Oregon Workers Alliance float in the 1937 Rose Festival Parade featured Martina Gangle Curl as Liberty. *Hank Curl.*

legislature and local government. Like many coalitions of the 1930s, the OCF suffered from disputes among its component organizations. Ben Osborne, secretary of the Oregon Federation of Labor, considered the OCF to be "influenced by the Communist Party" and a "back door to the CIO," which was the AFL's new industrial union challenger. On the other hand, the **Oregon Socialist Party** 40 withdrew from the OCF in 1938 because the Socialists charged it had become an appendage to the Democratic Party and made deals with capitalist politicians.

77 HARRY GROSS

Radical attorney **Harry Gross** (1902–1938) was active in the **OCF** 76, representing CIO labor organizers and other radicals until his sudden death from a heart attack at a young age. At his funeral, former Governor Oswald West noted that Gross "would have been a wealthy man if he had chosen to serve Mannon instead of the poor and oppressed." Three judges as well as future Federal Judge Gus Solomon and two city commissioners (Ralph Clyde and Jake Bennett) were among the honorary pallbearers at his funeral.

78 THE ABRAHAM LINCOLN BRIGADE 🌐

At least eleven Oregon volunteers joined the **Abraham Lincoln Brigade** to defend the Spanish Republic against a fascist invasion backed by Hitler and Mussolini between 1936 and 1939. One who gave his life

Harry Gross was a radical attorney in Portland until his death at the age of thirty-six in 1938. This picture was taken March 14, 1932, and kept by the Red Squad. *City of Portland Archives, A2001- 074.17.*

to fight fascism was William Newton Miller, who grew up on a farm near Dayton, Oregon, and joined the Communist Party in Portland. Miller was killed at age twenty-five in one of the last battles of the Lincoln Brigade. Before going to Spain, he was the roommate of Harry Wayland Randall, another Lincoln Brigade member and a 1937 Reed College graduate. Carl Lee Bellows, a Klamath Falls CIO union organizer, and Martin David "Toivo" Maki, originally from Astoria, were both wounded while fighting in the Brigade. Other Oregonians who went to Spain were Virgil Lanny Morris (a seaman and member of the National Maritime Union), Thomas Allen Norton (a poet, writer, and a Reed College student), Len Fletcher Spencer (also of Klamath Falls), and Harold Spring (a young Communist who died

LOYALIST SPAIN IS NOT DEFEATED

AMERICANS!!
Liberty & Democracy Calls You
HEAR OFFICIAL
Spanish Republic Delegation

Carmen Meana
Brilliant Young Social Worker and Spanish Trade Unionist

Jose Bergamin
Prominent Catholic Layman and Catholic Editor and Writer

Hear the Story of Spain from Spain's own Lips

| For the Cause of Loyalist Spain | **Civic Auditorium** **SUNDAY** **May 1, 1938, 3 P.M.** | For World Democracy and Lasting Peace |

Democratic America Greets Democratic Spain

Ramon Sender
World Famous Novelist "Counter Attack in Spain" "Seven Red Sundays"

Should America Help Hitler While Refusing Aid to Spain?
Can Democratic Spain Defeat German-Italian Invasion?
Hear the Answers! ! !

Auspices: Medical Bureau and North American Committee to Aid Spanish Democracy, and Portland Committee to Welcome Spanish Loyalist Delegation.

INSTEAD OF BERLIN AND ROME

(Left margin: SEND AMERICAN SUPPLIES TO BARCELONA)
(Right margin: LIFT THE EMBARGO ON SPANISH DEMOCRACY)

This flier called Americans to support the Spanish fight against fascism and to hear Spaniards speak in May of 1938. *City of Portland Archives, A2001-074.*

while fighting fascism in Italy with the U.S. Army in World War II). Earl Clyde Steward of Irrigon in Morrow County also fought with the Abraham Lincoln Brigade, and he, along with the others, was later called a premature anti-fascist. On his return from Spain, Steward lived at *3435 NE 79th Avenue*. When Carl Ralph Syvanen (who went to Spain from Astoria) died, Oscar and Julia Ruuttila placed this memorial in the *People's World*:

Carl Syvanen, veteran of the National Hunger March (1931) and the Abraham Lincoln Brigade, died as he wished with his carpenter's rule in his pocket and his hammer in his hand at Vancouver, Washington on July 23, 1969.

Captain Harry Johnson, a Portland ship captain, commanded several relief ships to Spain and personally presented a document signed by Helen Keller, Theodore Dreiser, and one thousand others pledging their commitment to Republican Spain. Portlanders raised money to send an ambulance to the Spanish government and on February 28, 1937, three thousand people filled the Portland Civic Auditorium at *222 SW Clay Street* (now Keller Auditorium), to honor representatives of the Spanish Republic.

Some Lincoln vets went to Spain from elsewhere but settled in Oregon later. Carl Geiser, the last combat vet who was a POW of the fascists, lived in Corvallis for many years and died there in 2009, the same year that Virginia Malbin, the last surviving veteran of the Lincoln Brigade in Oregon, died. Malbin went to Spain soon after her husband, Dr. Barney Malbin, went to work in the medical service.

She worked in Barcelona as a social worker assisting members of the international brigades but received firearms training. The couple later moved to Portland where Dr. Malbin joined **Kaiser Permanente 118**. Virginia was active the 1948 Oregon Progressive Party and together with other Lincoln vets, was welcomed to Spain by the post-Franco government.

The late Dell Hymes, a prominent anthropologist, had an uncle John Nelson Bowman, from his Portland family who died fighting against fascism in Spain. For a *festschrift* in honor of **Lloyd Reynolds 128**, Hymes submitted this poem:

> *Thirty Years War*
> My uncle, John Bowman, died in Spain
> And to his family. Black sheep, I
> And one loved aunt recall, believing
> History shears no worse than Portland.
> The nineteen-thirties did exist.

CHAPTER THREE:
Unions & Commies

79 BERT CANTOR 🎤

In 1937, Lincoln High School student **Bert Cantor** was interrogated by a member of the Portland Police **Red Squad 194** about his leadership of his school's chapter of the American Student Union (ASU). This chapter met in room 428 of the high school (now Lincoln Hall of Portland State University, *1200 SW Park Avenue*). The Red Squad officer was ordered to question Cantor by right-wing Portland school board member Louis Starr. Starr had declared that the ASU was a Communist organization and should be barred from Portland schools. The Squad officer accused Cantor of being a member of the Young Communist League and gave him a pamphlet entitled *Americanism or Communism?* But another school board member and 1924 Reed graduate, Harry Kenin, was outraged by Starr's link to the Red Squad and his attempt to intimidate Cantor, as was Lincoln principal Henry Gunn, who believed there was nothing wrong with the club. Cantor later joined labor attorney **Burl (B. A.) Green 73**, head of an early Oregon chapter of the **ACLU 123**, and other speakers to denounce the Red Squad at an ACLU meeting in the County Courthouse.

80 VALERY CHKALOV 🌐

Off the Lewis and Clark Highway at the Pearson Airpark, *1115 E. 5th Street* in Vancouver, Washington, is the only monument to heroes of the former Soviet Union in the United States. The monument commemorates the over-the-Pole flight of **Valery Chkalov** (for whom a street in Vancouver is named), Georgii Baidukov, and Alexander Belyakov. These men were the three Soviet fliers who flew over the North Pole in an Antonov-25 and landed in Vancouver on June 20, 1937. General George Marshall was commander of the Vancouver Barracks at the time, and his widow recalled that he asked Aaron Frank to send clothes for the flyers, who only had huge fur parkas when they landed. A Moscow-to-Vancouver committee tried and failed to raise funds for a monument in 1937, but one was finally erected in 1975. Portland businessman Alan Cole was awarded the Order of Friendship by Russian President Boris Yeltsin in 1996 for leading the private effort to erect the monument.

81 MINOR WHITE 🌐

The renowned photographer **Minor White** (1908–1976) lived on quaint *SW Cable Street* and at the old YMCA building when he photographed Portland scenes for the WPA in 1940. In 1938, he also was politically active as acting secretary of the People's Power League of Oregon, a militant public power advocacy group with an office in room 302 of the Oregon Building downtown. White also worked at the WPA Art Center in La Grande.

82 OREGON FEDERAL THEATER

The WPA's **Oregon Federal Theater** produced radical plays such as *One Third of a Nation* in 1938 at the former Elks' Club, *914 SW 10th Avenue*, now part of the Governor Hotel, where the **City Club of Portland** 167 meets.

83 DOROTHEA LANGE, ARTHUR ROTHSTEIN, & BILL LEE

The prominent Farm Security Administration photographers **Dorothea Lange**, **Arthur Rothstein**, and **Bill Lee** all documented Portland scenes, including Hooverville, traveling all over the state to produce a compelling portrait of late 1930s Oregon. Although over a thousand of the images are available at the Library of Congress, no comprehensive exhibit of that collection has been presented anywhere in the state

Arthur Rothstein took this photograph of a man living in a Portland Hooverville during the Depression, July 1936. *Library of Congress, LC-USF34-004817-E*

until the Oregon Cultural History Commission mounted many of Lange's Oregon photos in 2009.

Since Lange was working for the Farm Security Administration on her 1939 visit, almost every one of her 500-plus images were of rural and small-town Oregon. One, showing the then-common wood stacks for winter heating in front of Portland homes, was about the only exception.

84 RAY BECKER

Ray Becker (1900–1950) was the last of the nine **Wobblies** 17 imprisoned in the wake of the 1919 **Centralia Massacre** 39. From a "preacher family," he intended to become a "sky pilot" but joined the IWW instead. As the radical writer Anna Louise Strong's poem about Becker goes:

> But I figure
> The only practical Christians

TODAY
Are the IWW's
And the Socialists
And the folks
That are trying to get
A NEW WORLD!

Becker arrived in Portland after his sentence was commuted in 1939. Unlike his comrades, and despite the advice of his attorney **Irvin Goodman 71**, Becker refused an earlier-offered parole because he maintained his innocence. A large crowd of supporters greeted Becker at Union Station when he was finally freed in 1939, and he was welcomed at CIO headquarters in the **Governor Building 86**. A reception was planned at a Portland restaurant but, when organizers learned the restaurant refused to serve blacks, the event was moved to the Bohemian, then at *910 SW Washington Street*. **Julia Eaton Ruuttila 175** was Becker's close friend, and she became secretary of the Free Ray Becker Committee, established in 1936 by the CIO's International Woodworkers of America (IWA) union, whose Klamath Falls Local made Becker an honorary member. For publicity photos, Ruuttila wore a bracelet fashioned by Becker. After his release, Becker ran a small craft shop in Vancouver and lived in a cabin south of Portland until his death in 1950. At his funeral, Ruuttila put a red rose in his lapel — a tradition for old Wobblies.

85 JESSIE M. SHORT 🎙

Jessie M. Short was a member of the Portland school board from 1934 to 1937, the Federal Arts Committee, and also the city's Housing Code Committee for twenty years. She was also a professor of mathematics at Reed College until she retired in 1939. For focusing public attention on primitive housing conditions that maintained fat slumlord profits, as well as support of numerous progressive causes, the Police **Red Squad 194** called her a "Communist and dangerous radical."

86 THE GOVERNOR BUILDING 🎙

In the 1930s the **Governor Building** at *408 SW 2nd Avenue* hosted the offices of many working-class organizations. These included the state

The Governor Building hosted the offices of many working-class organizations during the 1930s. They included the state CIO and its newspaper, the IWA, the OWA, and the Portland May Day 1939 Action Committee. On the other end of the spectrum, the building had hosted the Ku Klux Klan in the 1920s. *Colin Smith.*

CIO and its newspaper, *Labor New Dealer* (room 314), the IWA (room 418), the dispatch office of the Marine Cooks & Stewards branch, the local chapter of the Harry Bridges Defense Committee (room 315 in 1939), the **OWA 75**, the Civic Emergency Federation, and the Portland May Day 1939 Action Committee (room 324). The Governor also housed the local Ku Klux Klan during the group's heyday in the 1920s.

87 COMMISSIONER RALPH C. CLYDE

One of the most outspoken proponents of a People's Utility District in the 1930s was **Portland City Commissioner Ralph C. Clyde**, often re-elected for his populist political outlook. He was first elected in 1931 and remained a council member until he died in 1943. He fought private utilities, supported labor unions, and his efforts were remembered in later attempts to reform Portland General Electric into a public utility.

88 THE GOLDEN PHEASANT

The Golden Pheasant restaurant, located on *SW 4th Avenue between Alder and Washington Streets*, was a favorite gathering place for liberal and radical Portlanders in the late 1930s. These radicals included the Oregon

On May 29, 1941, the Harry Bridges Defense Committee held a benefit dinner at the Governor Building. Morris H. Goodman, Mrs. MacGregor, and Mr. Rodman were identified and photographed by the Red Squad. *City of Portland Archives, A2001-074.83.*

Friends of China, the Progressive Municipal Political Club, and the **OCF 76**. The federation's executive secretary **Monroe Sweetland 76** (later a leader of the Democratic Party in Oregon) recalled that in the late 1930s, its poorly paid staff was often fed with a large bowl of noodles at The Golden Pheasant, courtesy of attorney Gus Solomon, one of the few in the political group with a steady income.

89 HARRY WILKES

Comrade **Harry Wilkes** (1889–1956) was a controversial radical who held leadership positions in many local radical organizations, including the Socialist, Communist, and Proletarian Parties. Known as "Poison Pen" for his furious attacks on capitalists as well other radicals with whom he disagreed, he was editor of the Portland-based *Western Socialist* before World War I, and the *Daily Workman* in New York from 1919 into the late 1920s.

Wilkes quit the Portland Soviet when it featured **Dr. Marie Equi 16** as a speaker at **Arion Hall 182** and quit the Socialist Party (which called him a traitor) to help establish the new Communist Party. In 1932, he accompanied James Ford, the black vice presidential candidate of the

Communist Party, and spoke at Ford's campaign meeting at the **Swiss Hall** 182. At various times in his checkered career, he was a government informer and quit, or was expelled by, various radical organizations.

1930s NOTES

1. Paul Dickson and Thomas B. Allen, *The Bonus Army: An American Epic* (New York: Walker and Company, 2005).

2. John Terry, *The Oregonian*, April 16, 2006.

3. For a discussion of her Portland years, see Helen C. Camp, *Iron in Her Soul: Elizabeth Gurley Flynn and the American Left* (Pullman, 1995).

4. Bunny Doar, interview. Gearhart, Oregon (1998).

5. Thanks to Julie Allen for introducing the author to Pele. Further reading: Pele deLappe, *A Passionate Journey Through Art and the Red Press* (Petaluma, CA, c. 1999).

6. The late Dr. William "Billy" Pilcher, Harry's son, returned to the Portland waterfront after an academic career as an anthropology professor. His doctoral thesis was published as *The Portland Longshoremen: A Dispersed Urban Community* (New York: Holt, Rinehart, and Winston, 1972).

7. Gary Murrell, *Iron Pants: Oregon Anti-New Deal Governor, Charles Henry Martin* (Seattle: Washington State University Press, 2000).

8. "A Small Vineyard," in "...*stained the water clear...*" (Reed College, 1966) 10-11.

9. *The Oregonian*, October 18, 1931.

10. Thanks to Peter Sleeth for Holbrook's article from The University of Oregon Library (*The Call Number* Fall, 1958).

11. Craig Wollner and W. Tracy Dillon (Eds). "Recollections of Tom Burns," *A Richer Harvest: The Literature of Work in the Pacific Northwest* (Corvallis, OR: Oregon State University Press, 1999).

12. June M. Benowitz, *Days of Discontent: American Women and Right-Wing Politics, 1933–1945* (DeKalb, IL: Northern Illinois University Press, 2002) 54–79.

13. They included future Lincoln Brigade vet Earl Steward, Esther Layton, secretary of the Portland League Against War and Fascism, Violet Olsen, Lillian Foster, Frank Webber, Lavena Bennett, Mary Gould, Seth Nordling, and Reed students John Hammond, Robert Lewis, and William Hood.

CHAPTER THREE:
Unions & Commies

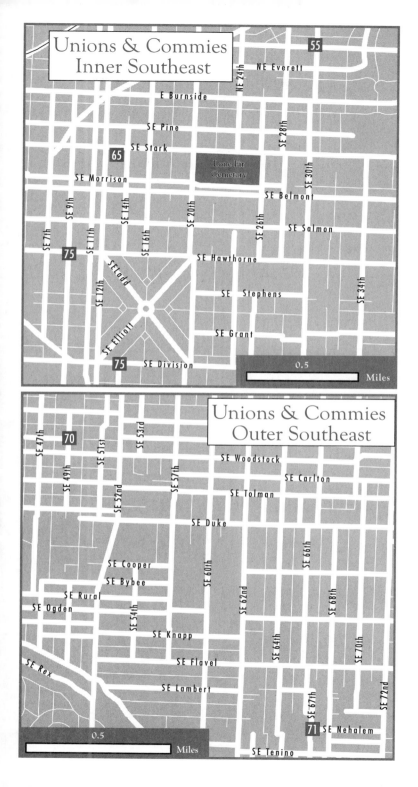

CHAPTER FOUR

McCarthyism & Cold War
WWII–1960

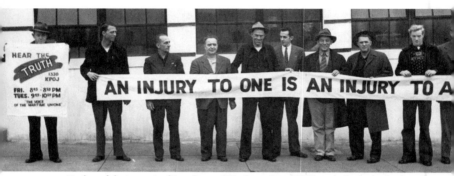

Members of the International Longshore and Warehouse Union (ILWU) on the Portland picket lines during the 1948 Pacific Coast longshore strike. Don Wollam, one of the Portland Four, is on the far left, and Jesse Stranahan is standing next to him. *ILWU Archives.*

Portland is ᴏᴋ except for being fifty years behind Seattle in
radical temper...
—Woody Guthrie, 1947[1]

W hen Nazi Germany invaded the Soviet Union seven months before Pearl Harbor, the Communist Left quickly shifted from opposition to U.S. participation in the European war to enthusiastic support for military action against fascism that lasted for the duration of World War II. Even after having sent about a dozen Oregonians—its "premature" anti-fascists—**to fight in Spain during the late 1930s 78**, until June 1941, the Communist Party was among many groups warning Americans against entering another imperialist war like World War I.

Thousands of Japanese-American Oregonians were herded behind barbed wire at the **Pacific International Livestock Exposition Building 96** following U.S. entry into the war. After being confined for the summer of 1942's sweltering months in the exposition building's foul-smelling animal stalls, they were shipped off—mainly to a concentration camp at Minidoka, Idaho. In 2006, Gresham was embarrassed when a memorial to its wartime mayor was cancelled when he was revealed as a racist opposed to the return of local citizens deported to concentration camps. He was not alone. A survey of businesses by the Portland Chamber of Commerce showed only two of one hundred and twenty-five answered "yes" to the question: "Should loyal Japanese be permitted to return to Pacific coast states during the war?"[2]

The wartime shipyards Henry Kaiser built in Portland and Vancouver transformed the city both economically and socially. But when thousands of black workers arrived in Portland to work in them, they were segregated into a Jim Crow "auxiliary" by Tommy Ray, head of the all-white **Boilermakers Union Local 72 103**. And all Portland black people faced tightened restrictions on housing and notorious "white trade only" signs on numerous retail and restaurant businesses. Some leftists worried that protests against such discrimination might divert their energy from the war effort.

Portland also became a major port for shipping lend-lease supplies to back the Soviet war effort, which was evidently a popular cause in the city. A November 8, 1941, *Oregon Journal* editorial over-enthusiastically celebrated the Bolshevik Revolution by describing a statue to John Reed that doesn't exist:

> Today, one of our great allies, the Union of Soviet Socialist Republics, celebrates the 25th anniversary of its founding. November 8, 1917, was the final day of the "10 days that shook the world," as they were named by Jack Reed of Portland, Oregon, whose statute stands in Red Square in Moscow and who is honored by the Russians as we honor great Europeans who helped America in its war for freedom.

The editorial concludes in boldface type:

> We of the U.S. can pause today to extend hands across the Bering Sea to a friend that has never failed to stand beside American democracy...

Communist Party activities in Portland during World War II emphasized the role of women and blacks in the war effort and as Communist political leaders. In 1942, the Multnomah County Communist Party held a "Daughters of America" birthday celebration for national party leaders Ella Reeve "Mother" Bloor, 75, and Anita Whitney, 80, at *721 SW 11th Avenue*. They called for attacks against German defenses in Western Europe as a "second front" to help the Soviet Union's struggle in the East. **Elizabeth Gurley Flynn 53** spoke to a May Day Victory Rally in 1943 sponsored by the Multnomah County Communist Party at **Redmen Hall 120**, which then was the state party headquarters. A few months later, in July, Communist Party National Chair **William Z. Foster 11**, speaking at a public meeting before two hundred and fifty people at Benson High School, urged labor unions to forgo their right to strike rule for the duration. American Youth for Democracy called upon young women to join "Sweethearts of Servicemen" (SOS), which proposed: "Let's get acquainted with other SOSers, to have parties and teas, knit or sew, go bowling and hiking, and do a little bit more to help win the war and bring him back sooner."

After the war, Flynn returned for May Day 1946, speaking against "the menace of World War III" at the Shattuck School on Broadway (now part of the Portland State University campus). For May Day 1948, Trinidad-native Claudia Jones, secretary of the Communist Party's Women's Commission, spoke at **Norse Hall** 182. Jones was an important spokesperson for black and women's rights—as well as a relentless critic of male chauvinism. In 1951 she was imprisoned together with Flynn and other national party leaders for "advocating the violent overthrow of the U.S. government" under the infamous Smith Act and later deported to England.

With victory in the war, the Left and labor coalitions that had supported the New Deal expected that its record of militant wartime patriotism would help gain it mass support in the political arena. But as a Cold War between the United States and the Soviet Union quickly became the dominant narrative of the postwar years, the American Communists' wartime ties to the "heroic" Soviet Union became a liability. The entire Left and labor coalition came under media suspicion as disloyal and subversive and became a target of massive government suppression.

The Old Left's final major effort was the originally hopeful **Progressive Party** 120 campaign of 1948, which was led by former vice president Henry Wallace. But he drew only three percent of the vote in Oregon (the Socialist Party received about one percent). An even greater blow to the nation's Left was delivered in Portland a few months later, when the Congress of Industrial Organizations' (CIO) tenth national convention met in Portland's Masonic Temple (today the Mark Building of the Portland Art Museum) and began the process of expelling most of its militant unions as "Communist-dominated." Some observers trace the disastrous decline of organized labor that continues into the twenty-first century to that decision.

The Left responded to the 1948 Vanport Flood with the **Citizens' Disaster Committee** 115 that demanded quicker and more generous assistance to flood victims, many of whom were black. Although by that

CHAPTER FOUR:
McCarthyism & Cold War

time Portland's leftists were already coming under heavy pressure from the growing McCarthyism movement, they nevertheless continued to lead the local struggle for racial justice through groups like the Oregon Civil Rights Congress. In fact, the Communist Party was the most fully integrated organization in Portland at the time

The low point of the McCarthy Era in Portland came in 1954 with the hearings of the **House Un-American Activities Committee (HUAC)** 128. A handful of informers named about forty-five Oregonians as Reds—most of whom lost their jobs unless they cooperated with the inquisitors. Four of them, known as the **Portland Four** 129, were convicted of contempt of court. By the end of the decade, McCarthyism had forced Portland's Old Left into an almost exclusively defensive position when liberal groups joined the McCarthyites by refusing to cooperate with leftists, even when they presumably shared objectives.

With radicals on the defensive, the role of attorneys willing and able to defend them became especially important. In addition to their dean, **Irvin Goodman** 71, among those who stood up were Reuben Lenske, Nels Peterson, Leo Levenson, Gerald Robinson, and Berkeley Lent. In 1959, a sign that McCarthyism was losing some steam came when the Oregon State Legislature by votes of 40–8 (House) and 25–2 (Senate) replaced the negative loyalty oath required of state employees with an oath to support the constitutions of Oregon and the U.S.

90 ARTHUR BOOSE 🎤

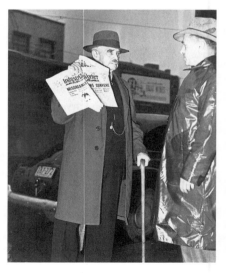

An old Wobbly, **Arthur Boose**, stood on the corner of *W. Burnside and 3rd Avenue* selling the Industrial Workers of the World (IWW) paper, *The Industrial Worker*, every Saturday for years through the 1940s. He was an energetic landscape painter. In

Wobbly Arthur Boose sold *The Industrial Worker*, the IWW newspaper, on the corner of W. Burnside Street and 3rd Avenue through the 1940s. *Oregon Historical Society, OrHi10695.*

2004, a posthumous exhibit of his newly discovered work was held at Artspace, a Bay City gallery on the Oregon Coast. The prominent Oregon writer Stewart Holbrook attended his funeral.

91 WOODY GUTHRIE 🎵

At the back of the four-unit house at *6111 SE 92nd Avenue* is the apartment where the iconic folksinger **Woody Guthrie** (1912–1967) lived during May and June of 1941. While there, he composed "Roll On, Columbia" and twenty-five other songs as an "information consultant" for the Bonneville Power Administration ("Roll On" originally included the politically incorrect line: "We [white settlers] hung every Injun with smoke in his gun"). When Guthrie left Portland in June to hitchhike back East, his first ride along the Columbia River was reportedly from attorney and future federal judge Gus Solomon.

His wife Mary stayed on to party, and it was here that their marriage ended. Guthrie soon returned to Portland in September 1941 with **Pete Seeger 179**, and they sang together at several union halls. In 1947, **Michael Loring 93** arranged a concert for Woody at Reed College. His final visit

Woody Guthrie lived at 6111 SE 92nd Avenue while writing his Columbia River songs. The sticker on his guitar reads "This Machine Kills Fascists." *NYWT&S Photograph Collection, Library of Congress, LC-USZ62-130859.*

CHAPTER FOUR: McCarthyism & Cold War

came in 1954 when, ill and destitute, he hitchhiked through town and was jailed overnight as a vagrant in Olympia, Washington.

In 1967, while Guthrie was in a hospital, Interior Secretary Stewart Udall sent him a commendation honoring him for his twenty-eight Columbia River songs and announced that the **Bonneville Power Administration Hood River Substation** 190 would be named in his honor "in recognition of the fine work you have done to make our people aware of their heritage and the land."

92 ELMER BUEHLER 🌳

Elmer Buehler (1911–2010) was a young Bonneville Power Administration (BPA) worker assigned to drive **Woody Guthrie** 91 around the Columbia River region for a few months in 1941 when Guthrie was on the payroll of the BPA to write songs in support of its dams and irrigation projects. During the McCarthy Era, Buehler helped save Guthrie's materials from destruction—ordered by the Interior Department—some of which he said he hid in the woodshed behind his home at *4606 NE 38th Avenue*. After retirement, which for Buehler stretched for decades during his 99-year life, he shared his detailed and entertaining recollections of his times with Woody, and was outraged when the Hood River Electric Co-op stripped Guthrie's name from its power sub station.

93 MICHAEL LORING 🌳

13045 SE Stark Street was the site of El Rancho Village, a roadhouse nightclub owned by radical musician and actor **Michael Loring** (1908–1993) after he moved to Portland during the 1940s to work as a publicist for the Bonneville Power Administration. His sister, Rose, had married the local leftist attorney Rueben Lenske. Loring was active in the folk music movement in New York City during the 1920s and 1930s where he introduced the folk anthem **"Joe Hill"** 19. He had worked with such folk luminaries as **Woody Guthrie** 91, **Pete Seeger** 179, Theo Bikel, and Carl Morris. Loring traveled with Henry Wallace on his 1948 presidential campaign trail and was a candidate on the **Oregon Progressive Party** 120 ticket for a House seat from Multnomah County. Later, until his retirement to the Oregon Coast in 1990, he was cantor at several temples in Fresno, California.

In early 1949, the Portland vice boss Jim Elkins played a joke on his protégé, County Sheriff Mike Elliott, tipping him off to illicit gambling

Michael Loring at the microphone at his El Rancho Roadhouse in 1949. Founding Kaiser Permanente doctors and their wives (from left to right): Frosty and Charlie Grossman, Virginia and Barney Malbin, and Nadja and Morris (Moe) Malbin. *Courtesy Charles Grossman.*

at El Rancho. Elliott sent a raiding party that was embarrassed to find a stag party of the "Footprinters," an equally embarrassed Portland police brass organization.[3]

94 *OSHU NIPPO* & OYAMA IWAO 🌳

On December 7, 1941, the FBI raided the offices of the Japanese-language weekly paper **Oshu Nippo** in the Merchant Hotel on *NW Davis between 2nd and 3rd Avenues.* The feds arrested its editor **Oyama Iwao** and confiscated its typesetting equipment. Today, the Oregon Nikkei Legacy Center is located at *121 NW 2nd Avenue.*

95 MINORU YASUI

In March 1942, **Minoru Yasui** (1916–1986), the first Japanese American to graduate from the University of Oregon Law School, was working late in his office in the former Foster Hotel (now the Musolf Manor Residence at *216 NW 3rd Avenue*). Determined to challenge a curfew order against American citizens of Japanese ancestry (which also applied to German and Italian nationals), he went into the street and demanded that the first police officer he saw arrest him. One officer declined, telling him, "Go home, sonny," but police headquarters finally obliged. He was tried, convicted, and sentenced to the Rocky Butte Jail. He was later sent to the Minidoka concentration camp, from which he was released in 1944 to move to Denver. From there, Yasui and Joe Grant Masaoka visited the Cheyenne jail to (unsuccessfully) persuade Japanese-American draft resisters from the Heart Mountain concentration camp held there to join the U.S. military. A controversial inquiry by Deborah Lim found that Yasui and Masaoka submitted their report on the resisters to the Japanese American Citizens League and the FBI.

96 1942 INTERNMENT OF JAPANESE AMERICANS 🌐

In February 1942, congressional hearings were held at the Federal Court House at 555 *SW Yamhill Street* in Portland on the need to deport Japanese American Oregonians to the camps. In contrast to significant opposition at the San Francisco and Seattle hearings, only one isolated voice was raised against the morality of the proposed deportations. It was that of **Azalia Emma Peet** of Gresham, a former Christian missionary in Japan. Peet asked, "What is it that makes it necessary for them to evacuate? Have they done anything? Is there anything in the history of this area to justify such a fear of them developing overnight?" She went on to challenge the need to deport the "law abiding, upright people of our community." The rest of Portland's religious, liberal, and radical communities were silent, although **Monroe Sweetland 76**, then

Portland's Japanese Americans were interned for the hot summer of 1942 at the animal barns of the Pacific International Livestock Exposition Building on N. Marine Drive. Four inmates died before the others, including a young Bill Naito, were transported to a permanent camp in Idaho. *Oregon Historical Society, OrHi28157.*

in Washington, D.C., expressed opposition. After the deportations, Portland attorney John Kendall managed funds and property for some of the deportees and preserved parts of their properties for their release.

So from May to September of 1942, the animal barns of the **Pacific International Livestock Exposition Building** at 2060 N. *Marine Drive* served as a temporary concentration camp for four thousand three hundred Japanese American Oregonians forcibly taken from their homes in Oregon west of Highway 97 and elsewhere in the Northwest. Henry Thiele's restaurant received a franchise to operate a satellite in the camp. After its infamous role in 1942, the livestock building reverted to its former use until the Expo Center replaced it in 1995.

One inmate recalled the horror of "the humiliation and the feeling of being treated like an animal. You couldn't stand it, the heat and the smell."[4] Another remembered gazing at the bright lights and hearing the cheerful crowds from the Jantzen Beach Amusement Park outside the barbed wire. On the other hand, Lois Sato, an inmate from Beaverton, wrote in the temporary concentration camp's newsletter *Evacuazette,* "It's not so bad as you may think, everything is new and clean. Food is good and plentiful. We may be guarded by soldiers, but we are hardly aware of them." Four inmates died before the rest (including the young Bill Naito) were transported to a permanent camp in Minidoka, Idaho, and elsewhere. In 1946, the first priority of the Oregon Civilian Production Administration was the restoration of the facilities to hold animals again.

CHAPTER FOUR:
McCarthyism & Cold War

97 CASCADE LOCKS CIVILIAN PUBLIC SERVICE CAMP #21

Several miles east of Cascade Locks off I-84 is the Wyeth campground, the unmarked site of **Cascade Locks Civilian Public Service Camp #21** that held conscientious objectors to World War II. The camp witnessed one of the few organized protests against transporting Japanese Americans to concentration camps when George Yamada, one of the 185 COs, was ordered to Minadoka in June, 1942. Many of his comrades, including future Oregon ACLU leader Charles Davis, signed protests that spread to other CPS camps around the country, including Waldport. Eventually, Yamada accepted transfer to a Colorado camp, but continued his nonviolent resistance to racism by participating in Congress of Racial Equality (CORE) actions with Bayard Rustin. He was finally released from prison in 1946.[5]

The former CCC camp at Cascades Lock housed conscientious objectors during World War II. *Courtesy of Lewis & Clark College Aubrey Watzek Library Archives & Special Collections.*

98 ROBERT & CARL DEIZ 🌐

Brothers **Robert (Ruby) and Carl Deiz**, both graduates of Franklin High School, were among the twelve black pilots from Oregon who became "Tuskegee Airmen"—the only black military pilots in World War II. The pilots were named for their training center in Alabama. Robert flew ninety-three missions in the European theater with the segregated 332nd Fighter Group and was the model for a 1943 War Bond poster, one of the few depicting a black person, which was distributed nationwide by the Treasury Department.

Robert and Carl were the sons of William and Elnora Deiz, who lived at *2254 SE 35th Place*. Their father came to Portland in 1914 to work as a waiter at the Portland Hotel and in 1923 became a dining car steward in charge of the Portland-to-Chicago run. Carl, the younger of the two brothers, married **Mercedes Lopez 140** in 1949.

Another Tuskegee airman, Charles Duke, became Portland's first black policeman hired under civil service. A veteran of the 100th Fighter Squadron, Duke lived at *7214 NE 9th Avenue*.

99 SAM MARKSON & RACISM IN VANPORT 🌐

The radical **Sam Markson** came to Portland from New York to work in the shipyards during World War II and lived in Vanport. In 1943, while on his way to visit a black friend, he was taken into custody by Multnomah Sheriff's Deputy Bob Henson who demanded to know Markson's political views and what he was doing in the "Negro section" of Vanport. Henson said that race riots would break out if white Southerners became aware of "fraternization." In September of 1946, a different sheriff's deputy shot and killed Bennie Sellers, a black Vanport resident. Two hundred community members, including Urban League leader Edwin Berry and leftist attorney **Irvin Goodman 71** met in protest, but, as usual, the perpetrator was exonerated.

After the war, Markson returned to his earlier trade as a sign painter, lived at *2924 NE 28th Avenue*, and was elected leader of the Portland Sign Painters Union. He refused to cooperate with the **HUAC 128** witch hunt in 1954 and was forced out of his union office in retaliation. His daughter, Karen Fine, testified that the experience devastated the lives of his family, as it did the families of many other HUAC victims, such as the **Portland Four 129**. Markson died in Portland in 1998.

100 THE RED FORT & LIEUTENANT NICOLAI REDIN 🏆

The Red Fort (or "Little Kremlin") was Portland's nickname for the former Wilcox Mansion and Rubenstein School of Music at *931 SW King Avenue* in which the Russian Purchasing Agency rented space during World War II. The Soviet Union and the United States were allies against the fascists at the time, and Portland was a major port for shipping supplies to the USSR. Some of the ships built in the Kaiser yards were leased to the Soviets. Originally launched with local names, they were renamed by their new operators. For example, the ship originally named the *Henry L. Corbett* became the Soviet *Alexander Minsky*. Future Senator Richard Neuberger described the scene: "Old-line Portlanders peered in awe from behind their brocaded curtains as the seafaring amazons [Soviet female ship captains] trudged in and out of the brownstone mansion the Soviet purchasing mission had taken over." On the other hand, Portlanders more supportive of our wartime ally organized the Russian American Club to entertain Soviet ship crews. After the war, a FBI informer (evidently erroneously) accused future Federal Judge Gus Solomon of belonging to it.[6] In April 1945, a Soviet seaman got drunk while on shore leave in Portland and hanged himself on board his ship, the *Drzuba* (friendship).

After the war, the United States charged one of the Portland purchasing staff, **Soviet Navy Lt. Nicolai Redin**, with espionage. He was acquitted after a trial in which he was defended by **Irvin Goodman** 71. We know that the FBI kept watch on the Red Fort because, when its reports became public many years later, they noted that then-Portland resident Regina Fischer, the mother of chess champion Bobby Fischer, had applied for a job with the agency and had joined the Communist Party in Portland in 1945. Bobby was two years old at the time.

Portland's Red Fort, also known as the former Wilcox Mansion and Rubenstein School of Music, stands at 931 SW King Avenue. Both the Red Squad and the FBI watched the house for Communist activity after World War II. *Colin Smith.*

101 WENDY ROSE IN THE JAMES AND JOYCE HARDER MEMORIAL PLAZA

The sculpture **Wendy Rose** is in the James and Joyce Harder Memorial Plaza at the east end of the Columbia River Waterfront Trail. The Plaza is named after owners of a metal fabrication company in the World War II Kaiser shipyard. The stainless steel sculpture honors all workers at Vancouver Shipyards, and was created by a group of local artists known as Women Who Weld. It presents Wendy Rose in work clothes set off by a red glass polka dot scarf. She is seen stepping from the home to the industrial work world and into the future, crossing the dam that powered the shipyards. She is surrounded by other local symbols of the era that help celebrate the spirit and legacy of the women of World War II.

102 THE JAPANESE AMERICAN CEMETERY

The Japanese American Cemetery at *NE 50th Avenue and Fremont Street* was the scene of American Legion and police threats against pacifists on August 14, 1943. Portlanders, organized by the pacifist Fellowship of Reconciliation, planned to clean up the cemetery for observation of the annual *Bon Matsuri* memorial for the dead by fellowship President Rev. J. W. Reed. Inmates of the concentration camp at Minidoka, Idaho, where most **Japanese Americans 96** from Portland had been sent, had donated thirty dollars to help pay for supplies needed for the clean-up. But Portland Post No. 1 Commander Joe DeBoest confronted Fred Willits and his cleanup crew at the gate of the cemetery, declared, "The American Legion won't stand for this monkey business," and started pushing Willits away from the gate. He was backed by Portland Police **Red Squad 194** Captain J. J. Keegan, who yelled, "That's the stand, Commander," and Multnomah County Sheriff Martin Pratt (Pratt had demanded the previous December that all Japanese Americans in Multnomah County pay their property taxes in advance because their property "will have disappeared before the close of another year"). Willits, supported by J. J. Hansaker, countered with, "We're here in a peaceful way and want no trouble for anyone," and said that "99 percent of Fellowship of Reconciliation members are active in Christian churches." Sheriff Pratt finally foiled the would-be clean-up by threatening the religious pacifists with arrest if they tried to enter the cemetery.

103 THE NEGRO SHIPYARD ORGANIZATION FOR VICTORY & THE BOILERMAKERS UNION

The Negro Shipyard Organization for Victory at the Kaiser shipyards protested their segregation from white members into the local union's auxiliary in 1943. As William McClendon observed: "Auxiliary unions are labor union officials' prized devices to render Negro workers helpless...[The Boilermakers auxiliary] is the most rotten form of white paternalism in existence" (*People's Observer*, July 16, 1943). Arnold Beichman and Cary McWilliams reported in the New York newspaper *PM*, exposing the Jim Crow practices of the **Boilermakers Union** under president Tommy Ray. Ray defended his racist policy by accusing Negro workers of having been used as scabs in a 1919 Portland shipyard strike. U.S. military intelligence considered the Negro Organization to be a "Communist front" and identified its president, Julius Rodriguez, and vice president, Walter Karrington, of being "colored members of the Communist Party."[7]

Fair Employment
Practice Committee

REQUEST NAMES OF ALL NEGROES DISCHARGED
BY THE KAISER CO., INC.

JULIUS RODRIQUEZ

President of the Shipyard Negro Organization for Victory,
recently returned from a Conference in Washington, D. C.
Giving a Report at a Meeting

Monday, August 16, 1943

—AT—

HUDSON HOUSE DORMITORY
N. E. LOUNGE A T 7:30 P. M.

If you have been discharged for non-payment
of dues, or for refusal to join the Boilermak-
er's Auxiliary, or if you have been re-employ-
ed in the yards, or secured other employment,
it makes no difference . . .

PLEASE BE PRESENT

The Negro Shipyard Organization for Victory protested being segregated from the all-white Boilermakers Union. This flier advertised a meeting in August 1943 where President Julius Rodriquez reported on a Washington, D.C., conference he had attended. *City of Portland Archives, A2001-074.*

104 CLARA PEOPLES & JUNETEENTH 1944 🌐

Shipyard worker **Clara Peoples** organized the first **Juneteenth** celebration at the World War II Kaiser shipyards on June 19, 1944. Juneteenth commemorates the day when word of the Emancipation Proclamation reached slaves in Texas, where it was traditionally celebrated and from where Peoples and many others had come to work in the shipyards. In

2010, a parade of trucks and cars carrying local elected officials, Miss Black Oregon, and a live band made its way down Martin Luther King Jr. Boulevard to NE Alberta Street, instead of the traditional location at threatened Jefferson High School. After the **Vanport Flood** 115, Peoples became one of the first black elevator operators in Portland (see site **109**).

105 WILLIAM H. MCCLENDON

William H. McClendon (1916–1996) lived at 2017 N. *Williams Avenue* after he came to Portland from Morehouse College in Atlanta in 1938. In that year, he founded one of Portland's most militant black newspapers, *The Portland Observer*, later the *People's Observer*, and finally *The Observer*, which continued until 1950 (a different paper with the same name founded in 1970 still continues publication). McClendon published a letter from "A Few Disgusted Negro Students" from Jefferson High School students in 1944 charging that they were told "No jitterbugging was allowed" at a school dance but that if they went to "a place designated for [them]…[they] could dance as [they] pleased." McClendon denounced the wartime racist policies of Tommy Ray's **Boilermakers Union** 103 and supported the **Progressive Party** 120 in 1948. He also operated McClendon's Cafe and Jazz Club, directed the Reed College Black Studies Program, and was Portland's NAACP leader in 1945. In 1943, military intelligence considered McClendon a "Communist Party organizer." It noted that his *People's Observer* "champions the Negro cause and protests the 'Jim Crow' aspect of Negro union affiliations," and that it was distributed through the Victory Bookstore and other Communist-front establishments.

106 GYPSY EXODUS, 1944 🌐

When upwards of one hundred **gypsies left Portland** for Texas at the end of 1944, it marked a success for Mayor Earl Riley's campaign of ethnic cleansing. He claimed the gypsies had come to Portland for war work but offered prostitution in vacant storefronts. Portland police and the Federal Security Agency, which maintained surveillance, challenged Riley's claim and reported that "there has never been a case of gypsy women being prostitutes although they may use the ruse to get a victim for fortune telling." Nevertheless, Riley persuaded *The Oregonian* to editorialize "Gypsy, go away" because "A gypsy is always a gypsy, and a gypsy is always a problem."[8] In order to deport his target population out of town, Riley had to procure a special ration of gas from the federal Office of Price Administration sufficient to fuel gypsy trailers all the way to Texas. Before the exodus, the deportees were called to gather at one of their homes at *616 NW 10th Avenue*.

Gypsies continued to live in Portland after World War II. According to Phil Stanford, Portland police under Mayor Fred Peterson charged them $500 a month to maintain a business and residence in storefronts along SW Front and First Avenues. By the mid 1950s, many Gypsy families had moved from downtown to SE 82nd Avenue and later to the Gresham area.

Gypsy children cool off at Skidmore Fountain during World War II, before they and their families were expelled from Portland. *Oregon Historical Society, Org Lot 667.*

107 DR. RUTH BARNETT

Naturopathic doctor **Ruth Barnett** (1892–1969) became a leading Portland abortionist when the city was a major center for women's health on the West Coast and beyond. Barnett claimed she had performed 40,000 abortions between 1918 and her retirement in 1968. Trained by Dr. Alys Bixby Griff, and **Dr. Marie Equi** 16, Barnett took over the clinic of Dr. Edgar Stewart in 1945, which occupied the entire eleventh floor of *The Oregonian*-owned Broadway Building at *715 SW Morrison Street*. After decades of paid protection from the Portland police, Barnett suffered her first arrest in 1951, when she was one of eight providers who were victims of a crackdown on "vice" by reform Mayor Dorothy McCullough Lee. Despite being jailed several more times in the 1950s and early 1960s, she maintained her belief in women's choice throughout her life. Her later offices were in the Jamaica Motel in downtown Portland, on SE McLoughlin Boulevard in Milwaukie, and at her home, which still stands at *2871 SW Champlain Drive.*

Dr. Ruth Barnett lived in this home at 2871 SW Champlain Drive in the West Hills. *Colin Smith.*

The Fair Rose campaign was started by students in the 1950s. Decals like this one denoted establishments that pledged not to discriminate. *Michael Munk.*

108 "WHITE TRADE ONLY" IN PORTLAND 🌐

One of architect Pietro Belluschi's lesser-known buildings in Portland was his 1946 **Waddle's Restaurant** near the Oregon side of the Interstate Bridge. Until its closing in 2004, Waddle's displayed its original slogan, "It's Time to Eat," on its prominent clock. But for blacks it was never time to eat at Waddles' or at many other Portland restaurants and businesses until many years had gone by. **The Coon Chicken Inn** at *5474 NE Sandy Boulevard* flaunted its racist façade for several decades until the early 1950s.[9] In 2004, it was bought and renamed Clyde's Prime Rib by Clyde Jenkins, a black man who is aware of its history.

According to retired Pullman steward Marcus Gordy, until 1938 the bronze drinking fountain at the south end of Union Station displayed a "Whites Only" sign. In the early 1950s, students from Portland organized a Fair Rose campaign, posting a decal at businesses that pledged not to discriminate.

Waddle's Restaurant operated from 1946 to 2004 in its prominent location next to the Interstate Bridge. Into the 1950s, a sign on the building read "White Trade Only — Please." *Oregon Historical Society, OrHi29161.*

109 VIRGINIA CAFÉ

In 1946, Esther Alene Grice (1923–2010) and **Clara Peoples 104** became the first black elevator operators in Portland when they were hired by the Eastern Department Store. Grice recalled that few downtown cafés would serve her. But the **Virginia Café**, originally opened in 1914 and located at *725 SW Park* until 2007 (now at *820 SW 10th Avenue*), and the lunch counter at the former Newberry's variety store at *SW 4th and Alder* were "open and even welcoming."

110 THE BLUE LAKE PARK PROTEST

In July 1946, the Young Democrats of Multnomah County organized a picnic at Blue Lake Park, but park manager Mrs. Paul Keeney barred three of the members because they were black. When the group protested her

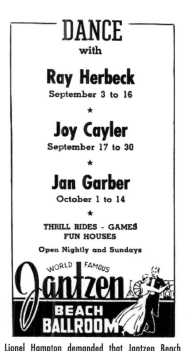

DANCE
with

Ray Herbeck
September 3 to 16

★

Joy Cayler
September 17 to 30

★

Jan Garber
October 1 to 14

★

**THRILL RIDES - GAMES
FUN HOUSES**

Open Nightly and Sundays

WORLD FAMOUS

Jantzen
BEACH
BALLROOM

Lionel Hampton demanded that Jantzen Beach Ballroom let down its color line before he would play in 1952.

racist action, Mrs. Keeney charged them with political partisanship and "stirring up racial prejudice." Young Democrats president Hugh Platt replied, "We do not urge the Negro people of Oregon to submit meekly to the established dictates of an intolerant few. We shall fight discrimination wherever we find it. And if that be 'stirring up racial prejudice,' Mrs. Keeney will have to make the most of it." A month later Platt was joined by the county Young Republicans at the Shattuck School to organize a "committee on civic unity" that would identify and act against racial discrimination. They were joined by representatives of the Urban League, NAACP, **Methodist Federation for Social Action** 133, the Brotherhood of Sleeping Car Porters, the American Veteran's Committee (by **Bob Canon** 128), the North Chapter of the Inter-Racial Fellowship, the Gona Street Community Club, and even **American Legion Post** 134 (by Herbert Schwab). They planned to name a citizen of Nisei and one of Chinese ancestry to the board at a later date.

The resistance of white Portlanders to integrate amusement and entertainment venues continued through the 1950s. In 1952, the manager of the Jantzen Beach Ballroom denied two black couples entrance to a public dance, as was the custom, until the leader of the orchestra, Lionel Hampton, was made aware of the racist discrimination. Hampton gave the manager two choices: make the black couples welcome or he would take his musicians home. The manager decided money came before enforcement of the color line and the couples were welcomed. [10]

111 THE PORTLAND ROSES & JESSE OWENS 🌳

The famous Olympic champion **Jesse Owens** (1913–1980) owned a black baseball team, the **Portland Roses** (sometimes called the Rosebuds), in

1946 at a time when the AAA Pacific Coast League Portland Beavers would only hire players who could at least "pass for white." The Roses were joined in the West Coast Negro Baseball Association by teams from Seattle, San Francisco, Oakland, Los Angeles, and San Diego. After opening against the Los Angeles White Sox at the Beaver's Vaughn Street ballpark (from 1901 until 1956, it stood between *NW 24th and 25th Avenues*) on June 4, the Roses played only about a dozen games before the new League collapsed at the end of July. On June 23, at Vaughn Street, Owens ran one hundred yards against time, gave a low hurdle exhibition, and raced four team members around the bases. The ballpark was built by C. F. Swigert, an owner of trolley lines that ran nearby. Today, his family's steel plant stands on its site with a plaque noting the former ballpark. The prominent sculptor Fred Lippman's statue of a steelworker (1969) is at *NW Vaughn and 25th Avenue*, near the original third base line.

Because the mayor and city council gave taxpayer money to the billionaire Paulson family, owners of both the Beavers and the professional soccer team, to renovate PGE Park for soccer only, the 109- year-old Portland Beavers baseball team left the city after the 2010 season.

112 BRIGADIER GENERAL EVANS F. & PEGGY CARLSON

U.S. Marine Corps **Brigadier General Evans F. Carlson** (1896–1947) enlisted in the Corps in Portland in 1922 and returned to live in Brightwood, Oregon, after World War II. He died at Legacy Emmanuel Hospital in 1947. He became a national hero for leading his Carlson's Raiders in one of the first assaults on a Japanese-held island in the Pacific early in the war. General Carlson popularized the slogan "Gung Ho" while assigned to China as President Roosevelt's personal correspondent in the 1930s. This slogan, which means "work together," was used by the Chinese People's Liberation Army. Because of his support for the Chinese Revolution and for his membership in the U.S. Committee for a Democratic Far Eastern Policy, he, like Army General "Vinegar Joe" Stillwell, became a victim of McCarthyism.

After his death, his widow, **Peggy Carlson**, who died in 1987, remained in Brightwood and was the **Progressive Party 120** candidate for Congress in 1948. In 1996, the Commandant of the Marine Corps, General C. C. Krulak, sent a glowing testimonial to a celebration of General Carlson's one hundredth birthday held by the Portland chapter of the Evans Carlson

Friends of the People's Republic of China. Krulak announced that the Marines, after decades of embarrassment, have rehabilitated the "Red General" and have joined China in claiming him as one of their own.

MICHAEL LORING
For the Legislature

JAMES R. CANON
For the State Senate

SHIRLEY M. HASKINS
For the Joint Clackamas-Multnomah Legislative District

ROBERT W. CANON
For the Legislature

HOMER L. OWEN
For the Legislature

FRANCIS J. MURNANE
For the Legislature

PAUL LEHMANN
For the Legislature

PEGGY T. CARLSON
For Congress
It's time for the People of Oregon to reclaim again the destinies of their state!
It's time to end the domination of the Lumber Barons, Eastern Capital, Private Power Utilities, and the Bank of America!
It's time to vote the monopolies out!

DOROTHY V. DRAKE
For the Legislature

Vote For These **PROGRESSIVES** *November 2nd!*

ESTUS H. CURRY
For the Legislature

Peggy Carlson ran for Congress in 1948 on the Progressive Party ticket. Her photo was listed along with the rest of the Party's slate of candidates in this flier. *Michael Munk.*

113 WARDELL HENDERSON

Wardell Henderson, a black war veteran, was executed in 1948 despite broad public protest that his trial was unfair. Accused of killing a white man in Vanport in 1945, Henderson was defended by **Irvin Goodman 71**, to whom he expressed his thanks and maintained his innocence in his last letter. "The Negro race shall never forget the massive injustice that was done to me," he wrote Goodman. "A lot of people are wondering how I can hold up after such injustice. Well I'll tell you why. It is because I am innocent."[11]

114 PORTLAND COLLEGE STUDENT 1948 DRAFT PROTESTS

About two hundred students from five Portland-area colleges held a protest meeting at the old **Jewish Community Center 185** to protest President

Truman's call for a Cold War draft in March 1948. Addressed by famed calligrapher **Lloyd Reynolds 128**, supported by the local Progressive Citizens of America, and led by Reed student (and future music professor) Bob Crowley, the singing demonstrators marched up Broadway. Vanport, Lewis & Clark, Multnomah College, Reed, the University of Portland, and the Museum Art School were represented.

115 THE CITIZENS' DISASTER COMMITTEE & THE VANPORT FLOOD 🎤

The Citizens' Disaster Committee was organized by **Progressive Party 120** supporters—including Nels Peterson, Vaughn Albertson, Victor Todd, Spencer Gill, Eustus Curry, and **Julia Ruuttila 175**—to demand city and state authorities provide more support to the eighteen thousand people, about one third of whom were black, left homeless when the Columbia River flood destroyed the wartime city of **Vanport in 1948**. During the war, Vanport had been the second largest city in Oregon. The Committee developed from the Vanport Tenants League and was supported by, among others, the Oregon Wallace for President Committee, the Oregon CIO council, and the Oregon Communist Party. It shared the office of the American Veterans Committee at *510 SW 2nd Avenue*.

The committee organized a mass meeting at Benson High School to demand city agencies move faster to provide integrated housing and other services to the flood refugees. **Paul Robeson 136**, who had visited Vanport in 1947, toured the site after the flood and at a Disaster Committee meeting at the former Holladay School (closed in 1969) observed "if someone had been more interested in human life than in profits, this wouldn't have happened." The Citizens' Committee gave a voice to residents when they complained to the city council that while business owners were warned to move their stock, authorities assured residents that the dikes would hold. Ex-Vanport College student Bruce Bishop, later editor of the International Woodworkers of America (IWA) union newspaper, told the council, "Just give the people of Vanport the chance to help themselves." A persistent rumor in the black community holds that many more than fifteen people died in the flood, as was officially reported. The rumors say other victims were secretly buried in the Terminal Ice and Cold Storage Company Building at the west end of the Steel Bridge. As also acknowledged after the 2005 New Orleans disaster, the Multnomah County Coroner admitted the possibility that

The Vanport Flood of 1948 displaced more than eighteen thousand people, nearly one third of them black, when the Columbia River destroyed the wartime city of Vanport. This photo shows two men, one carrying a small child away from the destruction. *City of Portland Archives, A2001-025.1208.*

CHAPTER FOUR:
McCarthyism & Cold War

The Vanport Flood caused the Progressive Party to organize the Citizens' Disaster Committee to demand more support from city and state officials for those who lost their homes. The Committee was supported by the Oregon CIO and the Communist Party, among others. *City of Portland Archives, A2001-078.*

not all bodies had been found. Some, he said, "may have been carried downriver."

The Portland Police **Red Squad** 194, now under the leadership of William "Big Boy" Browne, advised Oregon Governor John Hall to cancel a meeting with the Citizens' Committee because it was a subversive organization. Julia Ruuttila was fired from her job at the Oregon Public Welfare Commission because of her support for the objectives of the Committee and related activities.

116 POLICE MURDER AT GUILD'S LAKE COURTS

Guild's Lake Courts, not as well known as Vanport or Columbia Villas as wartime housing for shipyard workers, was the site of a notorious August, 1945 killing of Ervin Jones, an innocent black resident and father of five. Plain-clothes police looking for a murder suspect mistakenly raided his home in the middle of the night. Jones, believing thieves were breaking into his apartment, fired a warning shot into the ceiling and was shot and killed by detective Bard Purcell. Despite the efforts of leftist attorney **Irvin Goodman** 71, and the testimony of Jones's widow Elva (who had taken their children back to Louisiana after the killing) and her sister Susie Rambo, an all white coroner's jury—in an act familiar to Portlanders in most police killings—found the murder to be "justified homicide."

The cover-up roused members of the black community as well as Portland religious liberals and radicals. Led by President Rev. James Clow, Ruth Haefner of the NAACP, Rev. George Brown of the Gona Street Community church in Guild's Lake, Urban League director Erwin Berry, former member of Congress Nan Wood Honeyman, **Fern Gage** 186, leftists Goodman and Nels Peterson, and George Thomas of the Portland Council of Churches, the group demanded that Governor Earl Snell convene a grand jury. That jury also exonerated Purcell while the police denounced the protestors as "racial agitators."

The West Side of the Communist Party tried to organize Guild's Lake tenants after World War II to demand rent reductions, and **Julia Ruuttila** 175 exposed the deteriorating living conditions there after the 1948 Vanport Flood.

117 THE EGYPTIAN THEATER ♟

Destroyed since the first edition was published, the former **Egyptian**

Theater's decorative facade remained at 2517 NE MLK *Boulevard* for many years after the theater itself closed. In 1948, black movie patron A. N. Johnson demanded his fifty cents back when theater manager W. Graeper told him blacks were admitted only to the balcony and that he "couldn't buy a seat downstairs." Johnson was among the speakers at a meeting held in the Galilee Baptist Church to plan a campaign to end segregation in Portland theaters and also promote a municipal civil rights ordinance. Other participants included Edwin Berry of the Urban League (who later became its national leader), **Irvin Goodman** 71, Eustus Curry, who was a **Progressive Party** 120 legislative candidate, the NAACP, Oregon Civil Rights Congress, and the Frederick Douglass club of the Progressive Party. The Hal Spring Club of Oregon's Communist Party (named for a comrade in the **Lincoln Brigade** 78 who was later killed as a GI in Italy) organized a picket line around the theater, which briefly succeeded in persuading Mr. Graeper to abandon his Jim Crow policy. However, a counter-boycott by white moviegoers caused it to shut down for several weeks.

Goodman's draft of an anti-discrimination ordinance gathered broad support and was passed by the city council in February 1950, when Portland became only the second United States city to outlaw racial

The former Egyptian Theater stood until recently at 2517 NE MLK Boulevard. In 1948, black patron A. N. Johnson demanded his fifty cents back when he was told he could only sit in the balcony. It was many years before Johnson was allowed on the floor. *Colin Smith.*

CHAPTER FOUR:
McCarthyism & Cold War

discrimination in public accommodations. But, reflecting a dominant racist atmosphere in Portland, voters defeated it in a referendum.

The late Hollywood actor Paul Winfield recalled that he first became aware of racial discrimination in Portland's segregated theaters in the late 1940s.[12]

118 THE FIRST KAISER PERMANENTE CLINIC 🌳

The **first Kaiser Permanente clinic** in Portland was established in 1948 at *NE Broadway Street and 26th Avenue*. Part of the postwar Kaiser Permanente was originally founded in Vancouver in 1945. When the wartime Kaiser facilities in the Portland-Vancouver area closed, five former physicians—Charles Grossman, Morris (Moe) Malbin, Ernest Saward, Wallace Neighbor, and Walter Noehren—decided to try operating the Kaiser hospital and clinic under what was then a controversial pre-paid group-practice plan. **Abraham Lincoln Brigade 78** veterans Dr. Bernard Malbin and his wife Virginia joined them the following year. By 1950, opposition from the Multnomah County Medical Society to Kaiser Permanente as "socialized medicine" caused many potential members to stay away. But the mass enrollment of one thousand five hundred families from Harry Bridges' **International Longshore and Warehouse Union (ILWU) 57** saved the fledging nonprofit HMO (by 1952, 25 percent of their members were ILWU members). During the McCarthy Era, Kaiser Permanente lost two of its founders, Drs. Grossman and Malbin, when Dr. Saward claimed to rid it of "Marxists and Communists." Now a major health care provider in the Portland area, one of its physicians was elected president of the previously hostile Multnomah County Medical Association in 1996. And Dr. Grossman, one of the few Oregon physicians still in solo private practice, was honored at Grand Rounds at Emmanuel Hospital in 2005.

119 THE PORTLAND SCHOOL BOARD & THE LEFT 🌳

Portland school buildings were often rented by organizations of the local Left, so those seeking to support McCarthyism after World War II by suppressing political assembly pressured the **Portland School Board** to restrict its use to what it considered politically correct events. The issue came to a head in July 1948, when a member of the board, red baiter and *Oregon Labor Press* editor S. Eugene Allen, moved to bar any organization listed as "subversive" from renting or using any school property. Instead, Allen's colleagues, whom *The Oregonian* reported had just "spent an hour and half listening to members of the audience call each Communists," voted 6–1 to prevent the Oregon Civil Rights Congress from using the Irvington School at *1320 NE Brazee* to hear German Red Gerhard Eisler. But when Allen's proposal came up at the next month's meeting the board supported it 4–3 and later even Carey McWilliams was barred.

HENRY A. WALLACE
PROGRESSIVE CANDIDATE FOR
PRESIDENT
OF THE UNITED STATES

A Program for Oregon...

- Public Housing Program
- Development of Public Power
- Price Support for Farm Products
- State FEPC Bill
- Repeal of Anti-Labor Laws
- Expanded Educational Opportunities
- Protection of State Timber Lands
- Liberalized unemployment benefits and workman's compensation

PROGRESSIVE PARTY OF OREGON

CHAPTER FOUR:
McCarthyism & Cold War

The Progressive Party represented the last major political effort of the U.S. Left in the 1930s. This pamphlet, from the 1948 presidential season, states the party platform. The presidential ticket of Henry Wallace and Glen Taylor only drew fifteen thousand votes statewide, which some attributed to negative press coverage and attacks claiming a link between progressives and the Communist Party. *Michael Munk.*

120 THE PROGRESSIVE PARTY & REDMEN HALL 🌐

The Progressive Party, which represented the last major political effort of the U.S. Left in the 1930s, had its 1948 Oregon headquarters in the appropriately named **Redmen Hall**. Its national vice-chair, **Paul Robeson 136**, attended the organizing convention of the Oregon Progressive Party in 1948, staying at the home of Thomas Moore, the party's secretary, at *5112 SW Maplewood Road*. The convention nominated the national ticket of former Vice President Henry Wallace and Senator Glen Taylor (D-Idaho) to run against the Republicans, Democrats, and Dixiecrats. Several nominees for the Oregon legislature later won Democratic primary elections in Multnomah County. But all were defeated when

Wallace-Taylor drew only fifteen thousand votes for President state-wide. Many attribute the failure to attacks in the press charging that the Progressive Party was supported by the Communist Party. When asked about the turnout for one of his campaign stops at the Civic Auditorium in Portland, Wallace said, "Pretty good, considering Portland." His interviewer, a speechwriter friend, claimed his Portland appearance was "organized by a Communist-led union." "Well," Wallace observed, "they get out the crowds."[13] In September, *The Oregonian* made fun of Taylor, a former vaudevillian and still a slick guitar player, by telling readers he "clowned and orated through a two-hour-long speech at a Benson High School" during which he was "showered with flowers from women party followers." Perhaps the paper's editors were responding to Taylor's blaming "scare headlines" for the "current wave of anti-Communist hysteria sweeping the country."

By 1952, only 3,665 Oregonians voted for Vincent Hallinan and Charlotta Bass, the Progressive Party's last national ticket.

121 ROY NORENE 🌐

Between 1949 and 1952, the notorious Portland immigration service officer **Roy Norene**, who had earlier participated with the **Red Squad 194** in the failed effort to deport ILWU leader Harry Bridges, arrested ten foreign-born Portlanders for belonging to radical groups and recommended their deportation. They included **Hamish Scott MacKay 138**, William Mackie, Karolina Halverson, John Stenson, James Yecny (who was arrested at his home at *121 SE 7th Avenue*), and Casimiro Absolor. Norene succeeded in deporting MacKay and Mackie in 1960 despite the efforts of the **Oregon Committee for Protection of the Foreign Born 139**.

122 THE DALLES PINEAPPLE BEEF, 1949 🌐

During the ILWU's 1949 Hawaiian strike, in an event known as **"The Dalles Pineapple Beef,"** one ship loaded with pineapples made it to the West Coast but was turned away as "hot cargo" by longshoremen in Seattle and Tacoma. The ship's owners tried to sneak it down the Columbia River in the fog to non-union The Dalles, but the Portland local was alerted and sent hundreds of pickets to prevent unloading. When a strikebreakers' truck almost killed some longshoremen, it was attacked, overturned, and its two scabs beaten. One of them was about to be killed when Toby Christensen, a fighter veteran of the **1934 Maritime Strike 57**, saved him by knocking his fellow longshoreman out. The longshoremen threw most of the "hot" pineapples in the river and the Hawaiian Pineapple company later won damages from the ILWU. But two scab truckers got their pineapples into Portland and were about to load them into boxcars at the Southern Pacific freight depot at *NW 8th Avenue and Hoyt Street* when they were caught and set upon by six ILWU pickets who had eluded police guards. *The Oregonian* reported that the "fisticuffs climaxed a day of tension in which heavily armed squads of city police and state patrolmen sought to protect the two truckers, who were threatened repeatedly by a group of twenty-five to forty pickets who followed the trucks in a game of hide and seek around Portland's west side as they sought a safe haven to unload."

123 ALLAN HART & THE AMERICAN CIVIL LIBERTIES UNION 🎙

Liberal attorney **Allan Hart** (1909–2002), together with Gus Solomon and others, was one of the authors of a definitive 1938 expose of the Police **Red Squad 194**, produced by the Oregon chapter of the National Lawyers Guild. But by 1951, when some Portlanders attempted to revive a chapter of the **American Civil Liberties Union (ACLU)** to resist McCarthyism, Hart worked to prevent it, claiming that some of its proponents, such as Reuben Lenske and Nels Peterson, wanted it to become a front for the radical Civil Rights Congress. In November, Hart reported to the national ACLU office that thirty people attended a meeting in the Dekum Building at *519 SW 3rd Avenue* and debated whether to establish (or revive) a local chapter, and that it was defeated in a 15–15 tie vote.

Ironically, it was the liberal opposition to its leftist supporters that assured there would be no ACLU in Portland during the critical McCarthy Era.

124 BARBARA AMY HUDSON

Barbara Amy Hudson (1929–2008), a native Oregonian, lived the life of a progressive activist for labor reform, racial equality, and women's rights. With a PhD in

Barbara Hudson was a radical activist from her undergraduate days at Oregon State College to her later years with the Labor Round Table in Vancouver.

economic history with a dissertation on Douglas County, she was an itinerate teacher of economics, history, and women's studies at Portland State University, Portland Community College, Lewis & Clark College, Eastern Oregon University, and Clark College. Her impact was experienced by Ernest Warren, who, after graduating in the last class from the old Lincoln High School (now PSU's Lincoln Hall) in 1952, became one of the first black students at Oregon State College (now University). Barbara became part of his life when he tried to join a "Caucasians only" fraternity in Corvallis, and Barbara joined him in what he called a "premature" civil rights group called the "Cosmopolitan Club" to fight racism on campus. In the 1950s, Barbara and other opponents of racism were often called (sometimes accurately) "Communists." Her memorial meeting was held in the

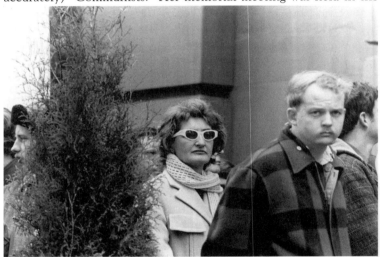

Rose Leopold was an active Portland radical for nearly fifty years. She organized a committee to save Julius and Ethel Rosenberg and was active in WILPF. Jon Kimball was also identified by the Red Squad in this photo which was taken at a peace rally in February of 1966. *City of Portland Archives, A2004-005.*

Vancouver Unitarian Universalist Church, *4505 East 18th Street.*

125 ROSE LEOPOLD & THE ROSENBERGS 🌳

Rose Leopold (1918–1995) arrived in Portland in 1951, a thirty-three-year-old New Yorker who had joined the Communist Party as a college student in the 1930s. She immediately plunged into local political activism by organizing a local committee in an effort to save accused Soviet spies Julius and Ethel Rosenberg from execution. She recalled that "the Jewish community was silent all over. They were scared shitless. Bernie (my husband) and I rented a big house [*1319 SE 32nd Place*] which became the center for the committee and our events... There was nothing else you could do in those times. The speakers spoke mostly at homes...We all expected the FBI. I knew my phone was tapped...The FBI did come to the door but I said 'I'm not talking to you.'" After the Rosenbergs' execution, Leopold wrote to supporters that the Rosenbergs' "integrity and splendor of purpose inspires the humanist, the progressive, and the radicals of this nation to continue the fight to clear their good name. We on this Committee to Secure Justice in the Rosenberg Case will do that and more." She continued to host leftist speakers and write protest letters against McCarthyism to the Portland papers. When **HUAC 128** came to town in 1954, she observed with sorrow that "there was such a terrible, dead silence... One weekend every progressive I knew went to the beach. They thought they might be called." Later, Leopold was active in the **Women's International League for Peace and Freedom (WILPF) 29**, the DoJump Theater, Red Rose School, and *The Portland Alliance*.[14]

126 GUILD THEATER & CENSORSHIP 🎙

For many years the **Board of Motion Picture and Entertainment Review** tried to keep Portlanders away from radical films. In 1940, for example, they banned the Soviet movie, *Professor Malmock*, which told the story of a Jewish doctor in Nazi Germany who fled to the Soviet Union. It was banned because the Board found it "offensive to a friendly power"—Nazi Germany! One Reed student, Jerome Radding, signed a petition protesting the ban and fifteen years later, as a doctor in a veteran's hospital, he was branded a security risk for his protest.[15] The censor board finally overstepped its bounds in 1953, after its effort to ban De Sica's classic, *The Bicycle Thief*, from showing at the

Andries Deinum, a film professor at Portland State University, protested censorship of Louis Malle's film, *The Lovers*, in 1960. He came to PSU after being fired by the University of Southern California for being called before HUAC. *Portland State University.*

Guild Theater at *1219 SW Park Avenue* was overturned by the courts. In the 1930s, the Guild's predecessor, the Studio Theater, was prevented by the censors from showing newsreels—previously not subject to review. Noting that the board members had found twenty-four objectionable scenes in the 1,853 films they had watched in the past two years, the board told the city council that "the cost in time and money [$5,000 annually] is too great for the results obtained." However in 1960, a state obscenity law allowed Mayor Terry Shrunk to demand that the Guild Theater cut two scenes from Louis Malle's film *The Lovers*. Theater manager Nancy Welch was arrested when she refused and leading Portland cultural figures, including PSU film professor Andries Deinum,

The Guild Theater, at 1219 SW Park Avenue, was the center of a storm over the 1953 censorship of the classic film, *The Bicycle Thief*. It was also the site of radical events from the 1930s to the 1960s. *Colin Smith.*

protested the censorship. The theater was closed in 2010, although a local cultural group hopes to open it for new uses.

127 DR. GEORGE EBEY

Former Portland public school leader **Dr. George Ebey** was hired away to be deputy school superintendent in Houston in 1952, but fired a year later after a Portlander, Virgil Holland, attacked Ebey as "soft on Communism." The Houston school board fired Ebey by a 4–3 vote not for any problems with his performance, but because he did not provide enough evidence that he "actively fought" Communism in the American Veterans Committee in California in 1946. Portlanders interviewed by the investigator for the Houston board expressed "indignation and amazement" at "having words put in our mouths" after assuring him that Dr. Ebey did not exhibit any "disloyal" behavior in Portland.

128 THE HOUSE UN-AMERICAN ACTIVITIES COMMITTEE & REED PROFESSORS MOORE AND REYNOLDS 🌐

The June 1954 hearings of the **HUAC** were held in what is now known as the Gus Solomon United States Courthouse between *SW 6th Avenue and Broadway*. HUAC's intent, as elsewhere during the McCarthy Era, was to expose and isolate dissident Oregonians. Its main informers were a former Reed College student, Homer Owen, and former Reed Dean of Students, Bob Canon, who together named about forty-five victims—many connected to Reed—as having been members of the Communist Party years before.[16] All of the suspects relied on the constitutional grounds for refusing to respond to interrogation about their political affiliations, and four of them, known as the **Portland Four 129**, were later convicted of contempt of Congress for their defiance. Most of those who refused to cooperate with HUAC were fired from their jobs, including William Lewis at Mitchell Brothers Truck Line and Professor Stanley Moore at Reed College, which also suspended world-renowned calligrapher **Lloyd Reynolds** from teaching his summer art history class. Reynolds refused to answer their political questions, including whether he had "ever made posters, graphic art things, and exhibits of that nature for the Communist Party while at Reed College." The college resisted efforts to reverse its decision to fire Moore for more than thirty years,

CHAPTER FOUR:
McCarthyism & Cold War

This above all: to thine own self be true
And it must follow as the night the day
Thou canst not then be false to any man

W I L L I A M · S H A K E S P E A R E · 'H A M L E T' I, III.

Lloyd

Lloyd Reynolds was one of many who refused to answer questions about his political affiliation when called before HUAC. This example of his calligraphy, a Shakespeare quotation, was given as a gift to Ruth Freeman Stovall for her $35 donation to *People's World*, the Communist newspaper, in the early 1950s. *Dennis Stovall.*

Prof. Reynolds and his attorney, Kneland Tanner, at his interrogation by HUAC in 1954.
Oregon Historical Society, OHS 014553.

and it was not until 1997, when Moore could not attend for health reasons, that he was finally invited back to campus.

The fear that dominated the McCarthy Era assured there would be little protest in Portland (with the exception of the academic components of Reed College) against HUAC. There was no **ACLU chapter 123**, but ironically, seventy members of the Multnomah County Young Republican Club, meeting in March at the Chamber of Commerce offices, voted unanimously to condemn "the investigation methods" of Senator McCarthy.

129 THE PORTLAND FOUR

The Portland Four, who lost their jobs, were arrested, and were convicted of contempt of Congress after refusing to cooperate with **HUAC 128**, were Herbert Simpson, a clerk at Inland Motor Freight; Donald Wollam, a part-time longshoreman; Tom Moore, a farm-supply businessman; and John MacKenzie, an assistant produce manager at Fred Meyer. In trials in today's Gus Solomon building, they were convicted because the politically biased Judge George Boldt in effect directed the jury to deliver a guilty verdict. They were all fired or lost their businesses, and their families endured years of harassment and unemployment, even though the charges were dropped in 1957 after three of them appealed to the U.S. Supreme Court, where the Justice Department admitted it made a mistake in prosecuting them. The Portland Four are all deceased, but each has some family members living in Portland.[17]

130 THE FAMILIES OF THE PORTLAND FOUR 🍃

The families of the **Portland Four** 129 were also victims of the McCarthy Era. The widow of John MacKenzie described the "crisis atmosphere" that permeated their "fortress home" at *6125 SE 86th Avenue.* Mary Mackenzie said they and their children withdrew from all political and most social activity because they feared the FBI and informers like John's fellow Reedie Homer Owen—the source of their troubles when he named John as a Communist before **HUAC 128.**[18] Looking back in 1998, Betty Wollam, widow of Don Wollam, recalled the atmosphere in Portland during the McCarthy Era. As a Communist active in left-ist unions, especially the Marine Cooks and Stewards branch at *127 W. Burnside Street,* she noticed that soon after the end of World War II, the local radio and press began giving "virulent anti-Communist sentiments" generous attention. The personal consequence was that "friends who had never said anything to you about your politics began to be a little sharp. Gradually old friends drifted away under pressure. By 1950, I don't believe I had a single friend left."[19] Their daughter, Cate Wollam, remembers that after her father vigorously challenged HUAC in 1954, chalk curses were written in front of their home at *3154 SE Salmon Street* and she couldn't go and play until her parents had "washed the nasty words off the sidewalk." When Tom Moore lost his farm supply business for failing to cooperate with HUAC, his son, Barron Moore, was sent to live on a farm and the family was forced to leave Portland and move to California.[20]

131 PORTLAND ART MUSEUM DEFIES HUAC

Portland's most celebrated artist, the late Michele Russo (1909–2004), whose studio was at *314 SW 9th Avenue,* was conveniently out of town and thus unable to be subpoenaed by **HUAC 128** in 1954, even though he was named as a Red by informer Robert Canon. Russo and his wife, Sally Healy, came to Portland from Connecticut where, because of his radical politics, he said, "I never had a job the FBI didn't try to get me fired from." They arrived in Portland after World War II and first lived in **Vanport** 115, where Russo registered to vote as a member of the **Progressive Party** 120. During the 1954 HUAC invasion of Portland, the FBI also tried

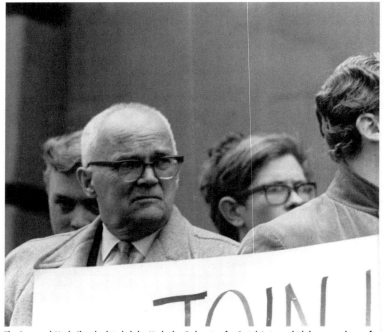

The Reverend Mark Chamberlain led the Methodist Federation for Social Action, which became a haven for dissenters and their views. He's shown here at a February 6, 1966, peace rally. *City of Portland Archives, A2004-005.*

to get him fired as an instructor at the **Portland Museum Art School**. But in a courageous exception to the behavior of other Portland educational institutions such as Reed College, the art school's dean, William Givler (1908–2000), himself a prominent artist, defied the visitors, FBI agents, who asked him to fire Russo. Givler replied that "everyone knows about Mike's politics" and defended Russo's right to continue teaching. Later, Givler and museum director Thomas Colt visited Russo at his home and assured him, "You are not vulnerable." Givler's action demonstrated that Portland employers could defy McCarthyism and were not required to capitulate.

132 THE HUNTERS & THE PORTLAND REALTY BOARD

In 1953, a cross was burned in the yard of a black family recently moved in a Parkrose neighborhood, despite the passage of "open housing" legislation earlier in the year. Two years later, after offering a $2,000 down payment, Navy petty officer **George Hunter** and his wife **Frances** tried to buy a home in the northeastern suburbs of Portland. Their offers were all refused. Finally, the president of the **Portland Realty Board**, Charles Paine, explained why. The Hunters were black, he pointed out, and the three hundred and sixty realtors in Portland had a "code of ethics which prohibits them from selling houses in white districts without the consent of the neighbors."

133 THE METHODIST FEDERATION FOR SOCIAL ACTION & REVEREND MARK CHAMBERLAIN 🎙

The **Methodist Federation for Social Action (MFSA)** in Gresham was led by the **Reverend Mark Chamberlain**, who was also a leader in the **Oregon Committee for Defense of the Foreign Born 139** and participated in the **ILWU's Bloody Thursday 57** commemorations. The MFSA was one of the few centers of resistance during the bleak McCarthy years of the 1950s. Through meetings, pamphlets, and preaching, Reverend Chamberlain, his wife, and a small group of committed Methodists and others provided a venue for dissenters and their causes. The federation's Sunday evening worship services and lecture programs were held at its meeting hall, *1910 NE Davis Street,* and occasionally would use the larger venue of the **Centenary-Wilbur Methodist Church 166.**

134 THE FRIENDLY FORUM

The Friendly Forum, which met in the cafeteria of the old YMCA building downtown, also provided an opportunity to hear dissenters during the McCarthy Era by holding regular lunches to hear mostly leftist speakers. They included visitors to the city such as artist Rockwell Kent, literary critic Annette Rubenstein, Mrs. Morton Sobell, Julian Schuman, and Ammon Hennacy, but also Portlanders such as attorney Reuben Lenske and peace activist **Fern Gage 186.**

135 THE OREGON COMMITTEE TO HALT NUCLEAR TESTING

In 1957, **The Oregon Committee to Halt Nuclear Testing** began by distributing pamphlets of Albert Schweitzer's plea against nuclear war to patrons of the former **Guild Theater 126** at *1219 SW Park Avenue,* which was then showing a film about Albert Schweitzer, the widely respected missionary and scientist. The committee was one of the first local peace organizations established during the Cold War by E. Wilton Hartzler of the American Friends Service Committee, Phyllis Johansen, wife of painter George Johansen, Helen Gordon of the **Jewish Community Center 185**, and myself, Michael Munk. The group raised funds for a full-page ad in a local newspaper and carried out a downtown petition drive against nuclear bomb testing. The Oregon Committee later joined with the national Committee for a Sane Nuclear Policy (SANE). Among its supporters were Rep. Edith Green, Maureen Neuberger, chemistry professor Arthur Livermore of Reed College, and representatives of the Unitarian, Methodist, and Christian churches.

136 PAUL ROBESON & SENATOR MARK HATFIELD 🏆

The last of **Paul Robeson's** many visits to Portland came in 1958 for one of his first public concerts after being blacklisted for his political views. It was sponsored by a leftist student group at Reed College and tickets were sold by the House of Sound, a record store in the heart of the city's black community at 3634 N. *Williams Avenue*. Indeed, black Portlanders made up more than one third of the overflow audience of over one thousand, with most of them making their first visit to the

Paul Robeson was a favorite of Portland's radical community. This snapshot, taken in March 1958, shows Robeson at his last local concert visit, talking to Dr. Charles Grossman, one of the last Portland physicians who still makes house calls. *Charles Grossman.*

college by trolley bus. The enthusiastic support for Robeson from the black community was in sharp contrast to the fear shown by Portland's music establishment (downtown music ticket outlets J. K. Gill and Sherman Clay refused to even display posters of Robeson, who had filled the Civic [now Keller] Auditorium many times before he was blacklisted). In the black community's business district on Williams Avenue, almost every store, bar, and beauty parlor proudly displayed it.

At least one of Robeson's visits to Oregon stirred up racism. Former **Senator Mark Hatfield** recalls that after a Robeson concert at Willamette University in 1942, Robeson and fellow artist Marian Anderson, who died in Portland in 1993 at the home of her nephew, Portland Symphony conductor James DePreist, were barred from staying overnight in any Salem hotels. Hatfield, then a Willamette student, drove Robeson to a Portland hotel—probably the Benson—where Anderson had previously been allowed to stay. Hatfield recalled that a photo of Robeson as a guest of Hatfield's fraternity before the 1942 concert was used by his opponents to red-bait him in the 1950 campaign, his first for the state legislature.

In a 2001 *Oregonian* article, Oregon State University star tailback Ken Simonton picked out Robeson (a star scholar and athlete at Rutgers University) as a "football scholar-baller who endured the nonsense long enough to open doors for a brother like myself…far beyond the playing field."

CHAPTER FOUR: McCarthyism & Cold War

137 LINUS PAULING ♀

The only Nobel Laureate awarded two prizes that were not shared with another recipient (Chemistry and Peace), **Linus Pauling** (1900–1994), lived in his mother's boarding house at 3945 SE Hawthorne

Linus Pauling, the only Nobel Laureate awarded two prizes that were not shared by another recipient, lived in his mother's boarding house at 3945 SE Hawthorne Boulevard. He was called "soft on Communism" by *The Oregonian*. *Library of Congress, LCUSZ62-76925.*

Boulevard from 1910 until he went to Oregon State Agricultural College (now Oregon State University) in Corvallis. He performed his first chemistry experiments in its basement while attending Washington High School. At his death, *The Oregonian* anointed Pauling "Oregon's Biggest Brain," but in 1954 during the McCarthy Era it joined much of the media by accusing him of "fuzzy thinking" for defending fellow scientist Robert Oppenheimer against accusations of disloyalty. In 1962, he challenged President John F. Kennedy to halt imminent U.S. nuclear tests. If JFK went ahead, Pauling warned him in a telegram, he would "go down in history as one of the most immoral men of all time and one of the greatest enemies of the human race." The Linus Pauling Institute at OSU continues his work in orthomolecular medicine and related fields.

138 HAMISH SCOTT MACKAY 🌐

At Portland International Airport on the evening of November 18, 1960, **Hamish Scott MacKay** was torn from the arms of his young sons by government agents, put on a plane, and deported to his native Canada. MacKay worked temporary jobs in the Portland area during the Depression, working on farms, in the woods, and in hop and wheat fields. Those experiences gradually radicalized him and he joined the **Oregon Workers Alliance (OWA)** 75. With the OWA, he picketed fascist ships on the Portland docks, joined the protests against the execution of **Ted Jordan** 52, and read Communist publications.

THE EXILE OF
HAMISH MacKAY and
WILLIAM MACKIE

"... now he is here, a man without papers or chattels, a penniless refugee in a borrowed coat ..."

Hamish Scott MacKay was deported to Canada in 1960 for his involvement with "radical" organizations in Portland like the OWA. This flier protested his persecution by the Portland red baiters. *Michael Munk.*

The long saga of MacKay's deportation began in 1936 when, while working on the Works Progress Administration (WPA) stream protection project on Johnson Creek, **Roy Norene 121**, head of the Portland office of the U.S. Immigration Service, came to MacKay's home at *5425 SE Henderson Street,* demanding to know whether he was a Communist.[21] However, Norene did not succeed in deporting MacKay until the McCarthy Era provided a more supportive environment.

Later, with the support of Oregon senators Morse and Hatfield, MacKay was free to return to Portland, but preferred to live in Vancouver, B.C., while making frequent visits to family and friends in Portland. Before his death in 1984, he asked to be buried at Skyline Memorial Gardens, *4101 SW Skyline Boulevard.* A hundred people, many of whom had helped him fight his deportation, attended his funeral. One of his honorary pallbearers was fellow political deportee **William Mackie 139.**

139 WILLIAM MACKIE & THE OREGON COMMITTEE FOR DEFENSE OF THE FOREIGN BORN

The Oregon Committee for Defense of the Foreign Born (sometimes called The Oregon Committee For Protection of the Foreign Born), working from *4616 SW Corbett Street,* was the main support of **MacKay 138** and other deportation targets of the local office of the U.S. Immigration Service. Continuing in his role of suppressing dissent from the foreign born in previous Red Scares, the notorious **Roy Norene 121** ordered the arrests of ten Oregonians in 1949 for having belonged to radical groups. In addition to MacKay, the police also arrested another former **OWA**

WILLIAM MACKIE

AN URGENT APPEAL
TO OUR FELLOW AMERICANS

Help Us to Prevent a World War Veteran from Being Exiled

William Mackie was deported due to the efforts of Roy Norene and others. He was eventually allowed to return to Portland with the help of Senators Morse and Hatfield. This flier tells his story. *Michael Munk.*

75 member, housepainter **William Mackie**, then living at *4326 N. Montana Avenue*, who came to Portland from Finland as a child, and Filipino Casimiro Absolor, an officer of the Cannery Workers Union. Both **Julia Ruuttila 175** and **Martina Gangle Curl 178** were active in the committee.

Mackie and MacKay were the only two among the ten who were eventually deported. Federal Judge Gus Solomon ruled that informers Robert Wilmot, former Portland newspaperman, and retired railroad worker Lee Knipe of Hillsboro, had provided "ample proof Mackie had been a Red," although he acknowledged that the Walter-McCarran Internal Security Act under which he would be deported was a "terrible law." With the help of Oregon senators Wayne Morse and Mark Hatfield, Mackie was allowed to return to Portland in 1976 after promising not to join leftist groups.

WORLD WAR II–1960 NOTES

1. *Daily People's World,* May 4, 1947.

2. Counter Intelligence Branch, G-2, Western Defense Command, Presidio of San Francisco, Summary of Subversive Situation. August 1, 1943. (Confidential).

3. Phil Stanford, *Portland Confidential* (2004), 92-3.

4. Interview with Tom Fujita, 2001.

5. See Charles David and Jeffrey Kovac, "Confrontation at the Locks: A Protest of Japanese Removal and Incarceration during World War II," *Oregon Historical Quarterly,* Winter, 2006.

6. Counter Intelligence Branch, G-2, Western Defense Command, Presidio of San Francisco, Summary of Subversive Situation. August 1, 1943. (Confidential).

7. Harry H. Stein, Gus J. Solomon, *Liberal Politics, Jews, and the Federal Courts* (Portland, OR: Oregon Historical Society Press, 2007) 74.

8. *The Oregonian,* December 28, 1944. Also see "How Portland Deported its Gypsies During World War II," *The Portland Alliance,* July 2001.

9. This was a chain founded in Salt Lake City in 1925, according to Psyche A. Williams-Forson's *Building Houses Out of Chicken Legs: Black Women, Food, and Power* (Chapel Hill, NC: The University of North Carolina Press, 2006). The book includes accounts of the chain's racist practices by Roy Hawkins, a former waiter.

10. Phil Stanford, *Portland Confidential,* 83.

11. From his letter published in *The Oregonian,* January 25, 1948.

12. *The Oregonian,* March 10, 2004.

13. Michael Straight, *After Long Silence* (New York: W. W. Norton & Co. Inc., 1983).

14. Interview by Sandy Polishuk, *The Portland Alliance,* February 1996.

15. Letter, *Reed Magazine,* November 1997.

16. Michael Munk, "Oregon Tests Academic Freedom in (Cold) Wartime: The Reed College Trustees versus Stanley Moore," *Oregon Historical Quarterly,* Fall 1996.

17. Also see Michael Munk, "McCarthyism Revisited," *Reed Magazine,* May 2006.

18. Mary MacKenzie, "Surviving the McCarthy Era: A Family Perspective," unpublished manuscript, 2006.

19. Interview by Janet Dietz, *The Portland Alliance,* June 1998.

20. See Mary MacKenzie, "Surviving. . ." for more on the Wollam and Moore families.

21. See excerpts from his diaries, edited by Michael Munk, in Craig Wollner and Tracy Dillon's *A Richer Harvest: The Literature of Work in the Pacific Northwest* (Corvallis, OR: Oregon State University Press, 1999).

McCarthyism & Cold War Downtown

Willamette River

Steel B...

NW Johnson

NW Irving

Hoyt 106 122

NW Glisan

NW 11th NW 10th NW 9th NW 8th

NW Flanders

NW 3rd NW 2nd

NW Everett

NW Davis 94

NW Park

NW Couch 94 NW 1st

NW Burnside 90 130

SW Ankeny

SW Ash

SW Oak

SW Pine

SW Washington

SW Stark

SW 3rd

SW Alder

SW 11th

107

SW 5th

123 115

SW 10th 108 SW Park

Pioneer Courthouse Square

96

SW Morrison

SW 1st

Naito Parkway

...erfront Park

SW Yamhill

Morrison Bridge

SW Broadway SW Taylor

SW Salmon

SW 2nd

3 128

SW Madi...

SW M...

0.5

Miles

McCarthyism & Cold War
Westside

Willamette Ri...

NW Front

NW Nicolai

NW Wilson

NW Vaughn

111

Hwy 30

NW Thurman

NW 25th

NW Raleigh

NW Pettygrove

NW 18th

NW Northrup

NW Lovejoy

NW 21st

NW Irving

NW 23rd

NW Glisan

NW Everett

SW King

W Burnside

SW Tichner

SW Morris

SW Champlain

107

SW St. Clair

SW Park

SW 20th

100

SW Tay...

SW Fairview

SW Kingston

SW Salmon

SW Madison

SW Main

W a s k i n g t o n

SW Jefferson

SW Canyon

SW Columbia

SW Market

P a r k

0.5

Mile

McCarthyism & Cold War
Inner Southeast

McCarthyism & Cold War
Outer Southeast

CHAPTER FIVE

PEACENIKS & CIVIL RIGHTS
1960–1973

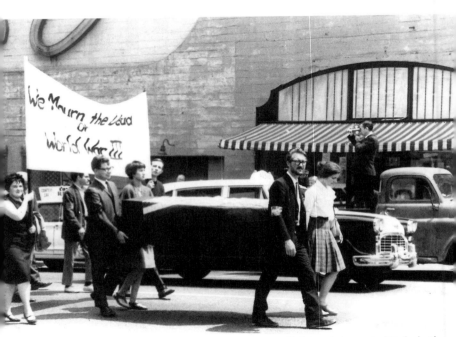

On July 5, 1966, the American Friends Service Committee walked through the streets of Portland with symbolic caskets. They were protesting U.S. involvement in Vietnam, or as they say on the sign, "World War III." Ace Hayes is the pallbearer looking at the camera. *City of Portland Archives, A2004-005.*

Portlanders participated vigorously in the two great social and political movements of the decade: the largely non-violent struggle for civil rights against the often violent institutions of racial segregation and discrimination and the frequently angry opposition to the massive U.S. intervention in the Vietnamese Civil War.

One of the few Communists still standing at the time, the late Susan Wheeler (1942–2006), helped to organize the city's largest civil rights march—eight thousand strong—to protest the 1965 police attacks on Martin Luther King's early march for civil rights in Selma, Alabama. Three years later, Portland's black community expressed its outrage at King's assassination in spontaneous street protests in which Portland police were accused of gratuitous **violence against black demonstrators 149**. The Portland chapter of the militant **Black Panther Party (BPP) 150** organized free breakfast, health, and dental programs, but its members were frequently harassed and arrested.

The transformation of earlier efforts for racial justice to the mass movement of the 1960s owed a debt to the Old Left's original efforts, as racists and the FBI who opposed the struggle acknowledged when they tried to marginalize civil rights leaders as "Communists." Wheeler and many of her comrades were active in the mass movement for which they had prepared the ground by their earlier work.

President Lyndon Johnson escalated President Kennedy's military intervention in the Vietnam War in 1964. Oregon Senator Wayne Morse was joined only by Alaska's Ernest Gruening in courageously exposing fraudulent claims and voting against the Senate's Tonkin Gulf Resolution, which provided a false justification for his full-scale invasion and occupation of South Vietnam and an air war against the North. Morse was eventually vindicated when the administration's factual basis for the resolution was exposed and the United States finally "cut and ran" from Vietnam in 1975 bearing responsibility for millions

CHAPTER FIVE:
Peaceniks & Civil Rights

of deaths. Later, Republican **Senator Mark Hatfield 136** also opposed the war, as did Oregon Representative Charles O. Porter. Opposition to the Vietnam War in Portland gathered steam through the 1960s but reached a climax in 1970 when students were killed by the National Guard in Ohio and by state police in Mississippi, leading to a **student strike at Portland State University 159** that was also attacked by Portland police. **Explosions intended to protest the war 162** occurred in city hall and military recruiting stations in Portland's east side.

If the remnants of the Old Left contributed to the civil rights movements and generally opposed the Vietnam War, leadership of the ultimately successful antiwar movement came primarily from a New Left—composed largely of youth and student groups such as the **Students for a Democratic Society (SDS) 145** who were inspired by and contributed to the twin movements of the 1960s. Although the SDS had its roots in the old Socialist Party, its revival in the 1960s was distinguished by their refusal to adopt the anti-Communist ethos of their McCarthy Era elders and by their preference for organizing anti-hierarchical community structures rather than electoral politics within a national political party.

Reflecting its distrust of anyone "over 30," the New Left showed little interest in the recommendations of the Old Left but struggled to define a radical ideology of its own. "We must name that system" that causes wars, racism, and poverty SDS leader Paul Potter famously declared to its first mass antiwar demonstration in 1965. But as an organization it never did, and instead gradually fragmented into feuding groups including some that urged violent confrontation with "The Establishment." Indeed, the roots of many later "identity" movements grew from objections to the straight white males of the New Left's original leadership. On the other hand, the demographics of that leadership reflected accurately the opposition to the draft by the war's domestic constituency. An effort to revive the SDS began in 2006, and the revived Reed Chapter published "The Fire Last Time," a brief history of their predecessors.

Other new political groups organized in Portland during this period were the Society for New Action Politics (SNAP) and two groups that adopted the Panther symbol (originally used by an Alabama voting rights effort): the **White Panthers 183** and the older Gray Panthers who continue to be active in Portland. There were perhaps a dozen locally-based, politically-themed collectives, communes, and groupings: the Portland Revolutionary Youth Movement, the Young Patriots (whose main group was in Eugene), Survival House, Red Emma, and others that went by informal names like "the Madison Women" (a group of women who moved together to Portland from Madison, Wisconsin). In 1969, the Portland Women's Union bought a former hotel at *SW Main and 11th Avenue* and converted it to the Martha Washington, a women's boarding house. In 2010, the Housing Authority of Portland remodeled it as a shelter for homeless and challenged persons.

A community of stores and services also grew to support the political/countercultural activists. Among them were the People's Food Store at *3029 SE 21st*, the Women's Health Clinic at *3537 SE Hawthorne*, A Women's Bookstore at *SE 25th and Ankeny*, short-lived Rude Girl Press at Reed College, Mountain Moving Cafe (a feminist-themed restaurant at *SE 39th and Stark*), and the Stomache (a collectively-run natural foods restaurant at *226 SW Main Street*).

In February 1970, the SDS-led (and the Student Mobilization Committee-supported) anti-military recruiting demonstrations at PSU culminated when about twenty students surrounded two U.S. Navy recruiters in the Smith Memorial Union. Four of them, Maureen Gray, Ileana Fenyo (wife of PSU Professor Mario Fenyo), Lynn Meyer, and Dan Wolf, made sure the recruiters left the building. For their direct action protest against the Vietnam War, the "PSU Four" were expelled from the University despite efforts of their lawyer **Don Chambers 176**.

Naturally, the revival of activism in the 1960s caused an expansion of the **Red Squad 194**, whose files were quickly filled with informer reports and photo surveillance of Portlanders exercising their political rights. They kept almost full-time watches at what they called "known militant communes" at *SE 47th Avenue and Bybee Boulevard* and at *SE 22nd Avenue and Ivon Street*.

> *While the races may stand side by side, whites stand on history's mountain and blacks stand on history's hollow. We must overcome unequal history before we can overcome unequal opportunity.*
> —President Lyndon Baines Johnson
> (shortly before his death in 1973)

CHAPTER FIVE:
Peaceniks & Civil Rights

140 JUDGE MERCEDES DEIZ 🌳

Before moving to Portland in 1948 and becoming the Northwest's first black judge, **Mercedes Deiz** (1917–2005) was active in the militant American Labor Party in New York as Mercedes Lopez Owens, daughter of a black Cuban father and a white Czech mother. She dated the prominent writer Ralph Ellison during "their salad days" in the late 1930s. "I remember sitting around with wonderful writers like Ellison and [Richard] Wright, listening and learning," she told a Portland interviewer in 1999. "I was so lucky to have that exposure to the great minds of the Harlem Renaissance."[1] She graduated from the Northwest College of Law (now Lewis & Clark Law School), managed Ben Anderson's law office, and in 1960 became the first black woman to be admitted to the Oregon State Bar.

But when she was appointed the same year to the Portland Youth Commission, the **Red Squad 194** reported that "leading Negro citizens are very displeased with the appointment and a representative of their groups is going to contact the Mayor regarding same." The Red Squad report went on to cite "rumors that she is still secretly in the movement" and that when Deiz was living in New York, "she was associated with and sympathetic to leftist movement," and led a local committee to defend Communist leader Claudia Jones.[2]

First elected Multnomah County Circuit Court Judge in 1972, she was re-elected to four consecutive six-year terms. A year after arriving in Portland in 1948 with a child and twelve dollars, she married former Tuskegee Airman **Carl Deiz 98**. They lived at *9340 N. Portsmouth Avenue.*

141 DANIEL J. JONES, BLACK CIVIL WAR VETERAN

The cottage at *2040 NE Rodney* was home to **Daniel J. Jones** (1843–1962), arguably the only black Civil War Veteran ever to live in Portland, was recognized as Oregon's oldest living resident when he died in 1962 at the age of 118.[3] Jones described himself as having been born a slave in Alabama and signed an affidavit when, at the age of one-hundred, he moved to Oregon in 1943, naming his place of birth, his parents, and his owners' names. He lived in Vanport until the 1948 **flood 115** and married his wife Hattie there in 1947. Ironically, he served with the Confederate army and fought in the battle of Petersburg, Virginia. He was survived by a stepdaughter, Mrs. Pauline Johnson. His wife died at seventy-nine, a month before he did. He is buried in Rose City cemetery.

142 PORTLAND'S NEWSPAPERS STRIKE 🌐

The old brick building at *1714 NW Overton Street* (formerly a Wells Fargo stable) was the home of the **Portland Reporter**. This daily newspaper was established in 1959 by journalists on strike against Sam Newhouse's *The Oregonian* and the Sam Jackson family's *Oregon Journal* and was published by Portland labor unions until 1964. The publishers tried to break the strike by importing scabs from outside Oregon, mainly from the South, and succeeded when too many journalists crossed picket lines and scabbed. One stanza of a prescient song written to support the strikers by workers in *The New York Times* composing room, sung to the tune of "Sweet Betsy from Pike," goes:

> "Sam Newhouse is clever," the publishers say,
> If he wins in Portland, they'll all have their day,
> Yes, if Portland goes under they never will stop
> Until the whole country is one open shop.

Despite the struggle of Portland unions, the way was cleared for the current monopoly of New York's Newhouse chain. Newhouse had bought *The Oregonian* in 1950 and paid $8 million for the *Journal* during the strike in 1961 only to abandon it in 1982 (the chain added the *Portland Business Journal* in 1995). In recent years, however, alternative papers such as the monthly **Portland Alliance**, which was not publishing regularly in 2010, **Willamette Week** and its predecessors, **Street Roots**, and even the relatively conservative weekly *Portland Tribune* have sprung up as occasional gadflies to *The Oregonian*. One consequence of its out-of-state-ownership and monopoly position is that *The Oregonian's* former slogan, "If it matters to Oregonians, it's in *The Oregonian*," has often suffered well-deserved ridicule when scooped on major local stories, including scandals of politicians such as Senator Robert Packwood, big businesses such as Portland General Electric, and corrupt government institutions such as the Portland

CHAPTER FIVE:
Peaceniks & Civil Rights

PROJECT OF THE OREGON COALITION OF ALTERNATIVE HUMAN SERVICES

the ALLIANCE

10 The Dekum Building   519 SW 3rd   Portland, Oregon   97204   (503) 222-4479

Original Alliance masthead.

Police **Red Squad** 194. In recent years, competition from electronic media has seriously downsized what used to be known as "the Big O" as it has most print media.

143 BERNARD JOLLES 🌐

In 1963, the Oregon State Bar denied admission to **Bernard Jolles** on the grounds that he failed to meet its moral standards by having belonged to the Communist Party. In 1956, Jolles had moved to Portland from New York, where he had been a longshoreman, and later graduated from the Northwest College of Law (now Lewis & Clark Law School) with top honors. After several appeals, the Oregon Supreme Court ordered his admission and Attorney Jolles was finally able to practice his profession. He practiced law so well, in fact, that in 1988, he was elected president of the Oregon State Bar. His office is at *721 SW Oak Street*.

Earlier, the Bar also denied admission to Frank V. Patterson, another Northwest College of Law graduate, because he refused to cooperate with the **House Un-American Activities Committee (HUAC)** 128 when it held hearings in Portland in 1954. Patterson was also eventually admitted.

144 FREDERICK L. SCHUMAN

In July 1963, over a year before the infamous Tonkin Gulf Resolution, Portland State College (which became Portland State University in 1969) visiting political science professor **Frederick L. Schuman** (later a regular member of the faculty) made what was arguably the first speech in Oregon against U.S. military intervention by President John F. Kennedy in the then little-noticed Vietnamese Civil War.

145 STUDENTS FOR A DEMOCRATIC SOCIETY (SDS) 🌐

SDS was first organized in Portland in 1964 in a house at *6008 SE 55th Avenue* at Woodstock Boulevard. Led by Reedies Jeremy Brecher, Phil Wikelund, and Mike Athag, it focused on organizing college students for antiwar and draft actions. One of their recruits at a fundraising party for the *Portland Reporter* was the future "Marxist environmentalist" Mike Davis. Future historian of the Left Maurice Isserman joined several years later when he came to Reed.

146 SUBVERSIVE ACTIVITIES CONTROL BOARD (SACB) 1964

In contrast to the low-key opposition Portlanders expressed to **HUAC 128** ten years earlier, they found their voice when another relic of the McCarthy Era, the **Subversive Activities Control Board (SACB)** came to town in April 1964. Hundreds of protesters surrounded the same (today's Gus Solomon) U.S. courthouse used by **HUAC 128** in 1954, and over a hundred Portland area college faculty and staff signed their names to a large protest ad in *The Oregonian*. The board was established under the McCarran Internal Security Act of 1950 and required persons it designated as Communists to register as such—making them subject to arrest and deportation to concentration camps (also authorized under the legislation) in the event of a national emergency.

Like HUAC, the SACB relied on paid informers to identify its targets. In 1964 in Portland, the informers were David and Norma Reilly. David was a youthful leftist whose background got him in trouble in the army and in his post office work. He said "to prove I'm not disloyal," he "volunteered" to become a paid FBI informer and joined the Communist Party in 1958. After their testimony "outed" them, they related their role as hosts to Communist meetings in their home at *4135 SE 29th Avenue*. The Reilys named two Portlanders, retired carpenter Norman Haaland and Navy veteran Ben Jacobson, who were both defended by attorney Nels Peterson. In 1968, the U.S. Supreme Court ruled the registration provisions of the McCarran Act unconstitutional.

Mayor of Portland from 1948 to 1952, Dorothy McCullough Lee, who welcomed advice from the **Red Squad 194**, was appointed to the SACB by President Eisenhower and served until 1962. In addition to crusading against vice, Lee was a dedicated Cold Warrior who advised Portland women in 1959 that "the best way housewives can combat communism is to see that the reputation of their communities is as spick and span as the inside of their homes" (*Oregon Journal*, 1959). The sensationalist (and sexist) "expose" book, *USA Confidential* (1952) called Lee, "a living monument to the folly of electing women to public office."

147 ALLEN GINSBERG 🎤

The earliest known recording of "Howl," poet **Allen Ginsberg's** best known work, was found in the Reed College library in 2008 by John Suiter while he was researching a biography of Reedie Gary Snyder. Snyder and Ginsberg had made the recording during a visit to Reed in 1956.

Ginsberg is believed to have stayed in Mrs. Alice Strong's garden cottage at 2525 *SW Montgomery* for several months in the 1960s, when his attendance at an August, 1965 Beatles concert at the Memorial Coliseum inspired a poem, "Portland Coliseum," in which he describes it as the "New World Auditorium" filled with a "red sweatered ecstasy" contained by a police line.[4] His appearance at PSU in 1967 caused the student paper to be shut down by PSU president Bradford Millard for publishing a nude photo of the poet.

148 RUSSELL KRUEGER AND HUAC'S FINAL ATTACK ON PORTLAND LEFTIES

One of HUAC's final efforts to suppress Portland's Left came in 1967, when **Russell Krueger**, among the last of the McCarthy Era's local corps of paid informers, testified before HUAC in Washington, D.C., about his undercover role for the FBI at PSU and Reed College. Krueger said he joined the Communist Party in December 1963 and reported to the FBI until October 1964. Like former Reed student Homer Owen who named fellow students before **HUAC 128** in 1954, and David Reily who named two before the SACB in 1964, Krueger accused about twenty-five PSU and Reed students of having belonged to party youth clubs at the colleges and one "downtown," but only Joe Uris, Denise Jacobson (whose husband was named by Reily), James Berland, and John Van Hyning were named in HUAC press reports. He also named many others as members of the Fair Play for Cuba Committee, Reed College and PSU Students for Peace and Students for Civil Liberties, the W.E.B. Du Bois Club, the FOCUS Club at Reed (later the Political Affairs Club), and the Helsinki Youth Festival Committee. Photos taken of Portland demonstrations — most likely taken by the Portland Police **Red Squad 194** — constitute a useful list of historic sites associated with local peace and civil rights efforts. But at the HUAC hearing they were used to identify those Krueger named as Communists and radicals. Photos introduced in evidence included demonstrations at Reed College in 1961; on Hiroshima Day 1962; for civil rights on June 23, 1963, July 3, 1964, and September 28, 1964; against **SACB 146** in April 1964 and January 1965; against the Vietnam War at the Pioneer Post Office on February 20 and 27, 1965; and at the International Days of Protest on October 16, 1965. **Donald Hamerquist 146**, openly describing himself as an organizer for the Oregon Communist Party, said he "always thought

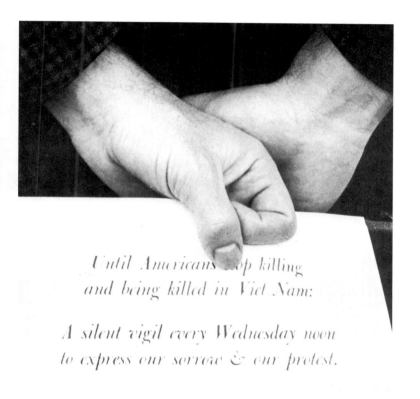

*Until Americans stop killing
and being killed in Viet Nam:*

*A silent vigil every Wednesday noon
to express our sorrow & our protest.*

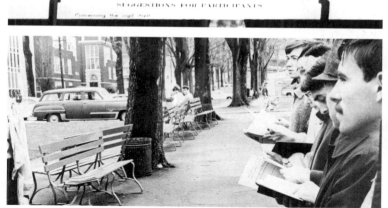

In the Park Blocks, sixty students kept a weekly peace vigil in the late 1960s. These images come from the PSU yearbook from 1967. *The Viking 1967.*

CHAPTER FIVE:
Peaceniks & Civil Rights

Joe Uris, shown in a photo from the 1967 Portland State University yearbook, was one of twenty-five students from the area named by Russell Krueger at HUAC hearings in Washington, D.C. *The Viking 1967.*

A political rally on August 30, 1967, turned into two nights of rioting in the Irvington neighborhood. Two to three hundred people caused tens of thousands of dollars in damage. *Oregon Historical Society, OrHi25045.*

Krueger was too clumsy and obvious to be an FBI informer."[5]

HUAC had become so notorious by 1969 that it changed its name to the "House Internal Security Committee." It was finally abolished in 1976.

149 CIVIL RIGHTS PROTESTS 🌐

Portland's black community experienced several serious street protests between 1967 and 1969. In June 1969, at least twenty fires were started along former NE Union Avenue (now MLK Boulevard). The formerly busy business district never recovered, and some lots remain vacant more than thirty-five years later. A Portland police officer, then in his twenties, remembers "standing at what was then *NE Union and Fremont Street.* Every building in my line of sight was on fire. There were people in the streets. I heard occasional gunfire." The Portland Police Department was accused of overreacting and that officer, the future Portland Mayor Tom Potter, admits the police department was not prepared. "We went out there with very little training, very little equipment and a huge gulf between us and the African American community."[6] That gulf had not narrowed sufficiently by 1981 to prevent a racist outburst by white police. Officers Craig Ward and Jim Galloway tossed four dead possums in front of the Burger Barn, a black-owned restaurant in Northeast Portland, and found support from hundreds of their fellow officers who marched on city hall in a successful protest to reverse their dismissal.

An even more outrageous racist police act occurred in 1985 when white officers Gary Barbour and Bruce Pantley killed Lloyd Stevenson, a black Fred Meyer security guard who had tried to cool a shoplifting confrontation in a Northeast 7-Eleven store. When Greg Cavic, a white man, began an argument with Stevenson, Barbour, backed by Pantley, applied a "sleeper hold," choking and killing Stevenson. On the day of Stevenson's funeral, two more white officers, Richard Montee and Paul Wikersham, added insult to injury. In the parking lot of the East Precinct, they sold about thirty T-shirts declaring, "Don't Choke 'Em, Smoke 'Em" to fellow officers. As in the infamous possum incident, none of the racist officers were punished despite large-scale public demonstrations. Mayor Bud Clark's effort to fire Montee and Wikersham was reversed and although a public inquest panel found Barbour and Pantley guilty of criminally negligent homicide, no grand jury would indict them. Barbour remained on the force as late as 1999.

150 BLACK PANTHER PARTY 🌐

The long history of racism among Portland police was one reason the Portland chapter of the **Black Panther Party for Self Defense** was organized on a revolutionary ideology that distinguished it from traditional civil rights organizations that sought racial equality under capitalism and believed that police behavior could be "reformed" with the hiring of more black officers.

The incident that launched the Portland chapter happened in 1969 at Lidio's, an Italian fast-food joint that stood at *NE Shaver and Union Avenue* (now MLK Boulevard). Neighborhood kids often gathered in an alley behind the shop for crap games and, just as Kent Ford was driving by, police were breaking up a game and had put a kid he knew in their patrol car. When Ford stopped and opened the car door to let the kid out, the police beat him up, arrested him and sent him to Rocky Butte Jail to await trial for "inciting a riot." In 2010, Multnomah County put on an exhibit in its old jail at *501 SE Hawthorne Boulevard* featuring artifacts from Ford's time spent there.

After ten days in jail, Ford was released on $80,000 bail, raised, he recalled, by "some Communists." In fact, it was **Don Hamerquist 146**, a former Reed student who had been recently expelled from the Communist Party for opposing the 1968 Soviet invasion of Czechoslovakia, who raised $40,000 from radiologist Moe Malbin, and an equal amount from Penny Sabin who put up Blue Bell potato chip stock. Nick Chaivoe succeeded in getting Ford acquitted and won a $5,000 civil award for the brutal treatment of his client. Ford and his former wife Sandra are parents of Patrice Lumumba Ford, a member of the "Portland Seven" serving time after being convicted in 2003 of traveling to support the Afghan Taliban.

When Portland police shot and wounded Albert Williams at the BPP's first office in 1970, a protest rally of hundreds downtown heard Nick Chaivoe, his lawyer, charge that the police had fired without justification.

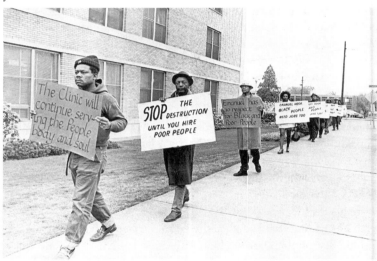

Portland's black community protested the expansion of Emanuel Hospital into the heart of their community. Frustration over being forced to continually make way for Portland's "progress" fueled these protests. *Oregon Historical Society, CN023743.*

151 PORTLAND CHAPTER OF THE BPP

On his release, Ford and several others, including Tommy Mills, Percy Hampton, Oscar Johnson, and Tom Venters, organized the **Portland chapter of the BPP**, with an office at *3819 NE Union Avenue* (now MLK Boulevard) at Cook Street. The original building is now gone. They recruited members outraged by police brutality, the use of black people as cannon fodder in Vietnam, and economic discrimination. The Panthers had the second floor of the building, while the ground floor housed The Resisters, a group that opposed the Vietnam War and helped potential draftees get train tickets to asylum in Canada. As Kent Ford remarked recently, the police "didn't like longhairs (the mainly white Resisters) and they didn't like Blacks." The site of its second office is an empty lot on NE MLK Boulevard south of Beech Street.

152 BPP FREE CHILDREN'S BREAKFAST PROGRAM

The Highland United Church of Christ, *4635 NE Ninth Avenue*, was the site of **the BPP free children's breakfast program** (later the George Jackson Memorial Free Breakfast program, named for another party leader killed in 1971 trying to escape from prison), which was the Panthers' first program in 1969. Every school day for eleven years, up to 125 children, mainly from Highland (now King) school at *4906 NE Sixth Avenue*, were served a filling meal: sweet rolls from Wonder Bread and ground beef from McDonalds, as well as healthy produce from Corno's and milk from Standard Dairy.

153 BPP'S FRED HAMPTON PEOPLE'S HEALTH CLINIC

The **BPP's Fred Hampton People's Health Clinic** at *109 N. Russell Street* at N. Vancouver Avenue was named to honor the party leader murdered in his bed by Chicago police in one of the FBI's notorious Counter Intelligence Programs (CONTELPRO) from 1969 to 1978. The building is now gone. Shortly after the breakfast program began, the Panthers planned a free health clinic. Hamerquist suggested that Kent Ford contact Jon Moscow, a recent Reed graduate and founder of the Portland Health Research and Action Project, and a writer for the *Willamette Bridge* newspaper.

The clinic was located in Dr. Webster Brown's former offices. The first physician recruited was Kaiser neurosurgeon George Barton, another Reedie. Sandra Ford, Kent Ford's wife at the time, did all the scheduling and was surprised she could raise money from Portlanders in wealthy neighborhoods in the West Hills. Eventually twenty-seven doctors (all white except pathologist Bill Davis, brother of the late actor Ossie Davis), plus nurses and medical students served between twenty-five and fifty patients every evening from 7 to 10 p.m. The FBI sent anonymous letters to Portland area doctors and dentists in an effort to sabotage the clinics. The clinic operated through the 1970s.

154 MALCOLM X DENTAL CLINIC 🍵

The BPP's first **Malcolm X Dental Clinic**, at *2337 N. Williams Avenue*, was opened in 1970, and Moscow helped again by recruiting dentist Gerry Morrell who was in charge of community outreach for the Multnomah County Dental Society. Sandra Ford was also scheduling for the dental clinic and even did a little "dental assisting." The Malcolm X Clinic, later moved to *214 N. Russell Street*, continues to serve dental patients under the auspices of OHSU Dental School, although the Dental School demanded in 1980 that the BPP leave the clinic.

155 CHARLES CX DEBIEW 🍵

A black Muslim minister, **Charles CX Debiew**, and his wife, Sister Iantha, opened the Temple of Islam in their home at *4056 N. Williams Avenue* in the early 1960s. In 1969, a more successful Mohammed's Mosque was established at *707 NE Fremont Street,* together with a school, a bean pie bakery, a café, and a fish market.

156 HO CHI MINH TRAIL

A path that skirts the freeway from Goose Hollow toward Portland State University was jokingly dubbed the **"Ho Chi Minh Trail"** by local antiwar and counterculture activists in the late 1960s.

This Rick Rubin drawing is from a 1982 calendar. It shows the Ho Chi Minh Trail leading toward the Portland city center. *Rick Rubin.*

157 THE FLOGGER 🍵

At the corner of *NW 25th Avenue and Vaughn Street* is a rare tribute to the American working class: **"The Flogger,"** sculptor Frederick Lippman's vision of a man swinging a sledgehammer. It was commissioned in 1969 by Ernest Swigert's steel mill and stands on its property (see **Portland Roses** 111).

158 WALLACE PRIESTLY

Wallace Priestly, an avowed Socialist representing the Ainsworth Park area of Northeast Portland, served in the state legislature from the late 1960s through the 1970s. Some of his political protests were especially dramatic. He jumped off the *Broadway Bridge* as part of the "Inner-Tube Navy" to protest warships coming for the Rose Festival and was arrested in Vancouver at the "White Train" protest against nuclear weapons transport. In the 1970s, radical attorney **Don Chambers 176** was his administrative assistant in the state legislature.

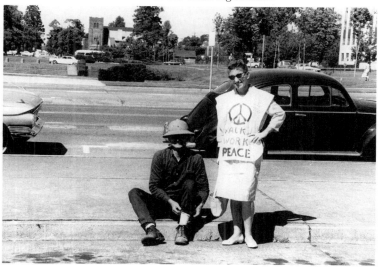

Wallace Priestly and Mary Jane Brewster at an August 6, 1966, peace walk. Protestors walked from Portland to Salem on Highway 99E. *City of Portland Archives, A2004-005.*

159 BATTLE OF THE PARK BLOCKS 🌐

In early May 1970, President Richard Nixon ordered U.S. troops to expand the Vietnam War by publicly invading neighboring Cambodia. Spontaneous protests broke out all over the nation, during which four students were killed by National Guard troops at Kent State University in Ohio and two by police at Jackson State University in Mississippi. In Portland on May 6, Portland State University students and faculty experienced the most powerful local event in the national outrage: hundreds went out on strike and the campus was closed for four days.

Gathering in the Park Blocks, demonstrators persuaded many other students and faculty to support the strike, and showed their outrage by blocking traffic with barricades built from park benches and debris from nearby construction sites.

On orders from Oregon Governor Tom McCall, PSU president Greg Wolfe reopened the university May 11. But when protesters refused a police order to take down a first aid tent, police dressed in riot gear attacked them in wedge formation with clubs. Almost thirty protesters were injured seriously enough to be hospitalized in what became known as the **Battle of the Park Blocks**. More than five thousand Portlanders marched on city hall to demand the organizers of the police riot—City Commissioner Francis Ivancie and Police Chief Donald McNamara— be punished.

In 1969, this peace march wound through downtown Portland, with tens of thousands participating. *Oregon Historical Society, OrHi23934.*

Years later, informed judgments of the event differ. Strike historian Dory Hylton noted there was plenty to protest against: the re-escalation and expansion of the Vietnam War, the shooting deaths of the Kent State and Jackson State students, the imprisonment of Black Panther Bobby Seale, and the shipment of nerve gas into Oregon. Hylton believes "the students were absolutely, 100 percent committed to non-violence."[7]

But PSU history professor David A. Horowitz, who supported the antiwar demonstration at the time, had second thoughts, suggesting that tactics such as the blocking of traffic and disrupting classes may have alienated the public. "If you're trying to change society for the better," he argued, "you have to have respect for the people you're trying to enroll in the changes, or you may end up marginalized."[8]

When Governor Tom McCall ordered PSU open on May 11, 1970, protestors refused to take down a first aid tent in the Park Blocks. The police, dressed in riot gear, attacked the protestors with clubs, and over thirty people were injured in what became known as the Battle of the Park Blocks. *The Viking 1970.*

Strike leader Doug Weiskopf, on the other hand, looks back without regrets. "I can't think of anything I'd [have] done differently," he says. "I was trying to make a point as loudly as I could and dramatically as I could. We got the message out, we made our point, and we made it pretty much violence- or vandalism-free."[9] And, referring to Horowitz as well as similar comments by Joe Uris, another student leader, Weiskopf laments, "What has made these tigers of the past suddenly wimp out and start whining about how we were wrong to be 'so angry' and to disturb the delicate sensibilities of an American public who would rather have ignored the horrors of the daily slaughter in Southeast Asia?"[10]

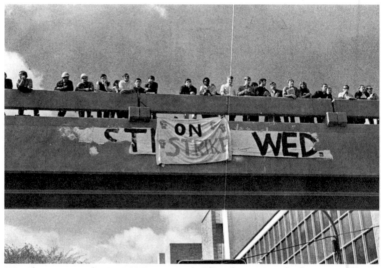

PSU students went on strike May 6, 1970, to protest the killing of Kent State and Jackson State students by the National Guard and police. The campus was closed for four days. *The Viking 1970.*

160 THE PEOPLE'S ARMY JAMBOREE & VORTEX I 🌐

The People's Army Jamboree was organized in the wake of the May **Battle of the Park Blocks 159** to counter an expected appearance by President Nixon at the August 1970 American Legion convention in Portland. But influential Portlanders worried about the potential for violence persuaded Governor Tom McCall and enough of its antiwar organizers to divert its potential protestors to a state-sponsored "little Woodstock" called **Vortex I**, held just outside Portland in Clackamas County and featured rock music. In hindsight, some observed that the event showed the ability of political leaders to significantly reduce an antiwar protest by tempting insufficiently ideological young people from political action by simply offering them a law enforcement-free good time.[11] Years later, it was revealed that the Portland Police **Red Squad** 194 had violated the rights of the original organizers with infiltration, wiretaps, and both secret and aggressively "in-your-face" surveillance. They also urged Portland newspaper publishers and station managers to slant their coverage against the protests by assigning only unsympathetic reporters and editors.[12]

The People's Army Jamboree, a protest group organized to counter an expected appearance by President Richard Nixon in Portland, was under heavy surveillance by the Red Squad. Ronald Betts was photographed at an August 31, 1970, rally. *City of Portland Archives, A2004-005.*

161 1970S HIPSTERS

Hipster protestors with a literary bent hung out at Reuben's 5 Peace and Pizza Tavern at *1239 SW Jefferson* in the early 1970s. Among the regulars were Mike McCusker, John Bertels, Art Honeyman, Wally Chambers, and Walt Curtis.

162 NORTHWEST LIBERATION FRONT (NLF)

Among the many radical groups that emerged from the New Left was the **Northwest Liberation Front (NLF)**, which the Portland Police **Red Squad** 194 claims was linked to the Weather Underground. Named for the line from Bob Dylan's 1965 "Subterranean Homesick Blues," "You don't need a weatherman/To know which way the wind blows," the weathermen (and women) were originally a faction within the **SDS** 145 that accepted violence as a political tactic while rejecting "white skin privilege" in an effort to support those they considered to be their allies, such as the **BPP** 150. The local NLF may have been responsible for blowing up a replica of the Liberty Bell outside city hall in November 1970 an act intended to recall the May "police riot" in the **Park Blocks** 159.

CHAPTER FIVE:
Peaceniks & Civil Rights

163 1970 LIBERTY BELL BOMBING AT CITY HALL

Weather Underground leaders Karen Lee Latimer and Jeff Jones were identified as operating underground in Oregon, and several others surrendered from hiding (and went to jail) in Portland, as did Katherine Ann Power in Lebanon in 1993. Weatherman Trim Bissell was arrested in Eugene in 1987 after hiding for seventeen years. Upon serving time in federal prison, he returned to Eugene and died there in 2002. Later, some activists motivated by the radical environmentalist ideology of the Earth Liberation Front pleaded guilty to arson against the property of twenty-first century lumber barons and other designated commercial enemies in Oregon.

There was an unsuccessful kidnapping of wealthy Portlander Ira Keller (of Keller Fountain and Keller Auditorium fame), whose investments funded the destruction of South Portland's Jewish and Italian neighborhoods in the name of "urban renewal," a robbery of a gun shop, and the Country Kitchen restaurant. The most violent act in Portland against the Vietnam War came when military recruiting centers at *4008 NE Union Avenue* (now MLK Boulevard) on January 2 and at *5030 SE Foster Road* on January 4, 1973, were damaged by bombs, an action intended to protest the U.S. bombing of a children's hospital in Hanoi, Vietnam. Several antiwar activists including PSU professor Frank Giese, who was fired by the PSU president after his indictment despite faculty protests, were convicted of conspiracy in connection with the bombings and served prison time. Memorial services for Giese (1916–2006) were held at River View Cemetery, *8421 SW Macadam Avenue*.

Frank Giese, a PSU professor, was convicted and served prison time for his connection with the NLF. He's shown here, in the center, marching with his wife, Jane, in a July 18, 1966, peace march. *City of Portland Archives, A2004-005.*

City Hall after a bomb damaged the Liberty Bell replica in 1970.

According to Lynn Meyer, Giese "was one of his comrades in the NLF." Among others were, James Cronin, James Akers, Robert McSherry, Leslie McKeel, Max Severin, and Chester Wallace.[13]

164 CHERYL JAMES

Cheryl Dawn James, a black seventeen-year-old Jefferson High School student, was imprisoned at the federal penitentiary at Terminal Island, Washington in 1971 on charges of assaulting FBI agents. In January 1971, several reportedly unidentified FBI agents burst into the family's home at *415 N. Jarrett Street* to arrest a twenty-year-old brother who was AWOL from the Navy. He maintained he left his unit to deal with a family emergency for which he had originally been granted leave. An FBI agent announced, along with a racist slur, "You're coming with us, boy." Cheryl was arrested and convicted when she defended her mother, whom the agents had thrown to the ground, by hitting one of them with a rolling pin.

A Cheryl James Defense Committee was formed, which included Stephen and Gretchen Kafoury, and was managed by **Julia Ruuttila 175**. It was among the many dissenting groups monitored by the Portland Police **Red Squad 194**.

CHAPTER FIVE:
Peaceniks & Civil Rights

1960–1973 NOTES

1. *Willamette Week,* June 9, 1999.

2. Intelligence Division Report, Portland Bureau of Police, August 15, 1960. Charley Trimble to Chief Hillbruner. "Confidential Information, Subject: Deiz, Mercedes."

3. Roy Roos, *The History of Albina* (2008), 152.

4. Reprinted from Mikal Gilmore, "And the Bank Played On," *New York Times,* August 24, 2005.

5. "Oregon Communist Leader Admits Inducting Informant," *Oregon Journal,* April 15, 1967.

6. "Potter on Riots, Redevelopments," *The Oregonian,* June 15, 2006.

7. "Four Days that Changed Portland," *Vanguard,* May 5, 2005.

8. Endnote 6.

9. Endnote 6.

10. "Years Later, Questions Unanswered," *Vanguard,* May 7, 2005.

11. Matt Love, *The Far Out Story of Vortex I,* (Pacific City, OR: Nestucca Spit Press, 2004).

12. Portland Bureau of Police Intelligence Report, February 10, 1972, from officer C. F. Trimble to Lt. Melvin Hulett, "Intelligence Planning, Functions and Critique of American Legion and People's Army Jamboree Activities."

13. http://www.livelogcity.com/users/copkiller11/434.html.

Peaceniks & Civil Rights Westside

NW 27th
NW 26th
157 NW Vaughn
Hwy 30
NW 25th
NW 24th
NW 23rd
NW Raleigh
NW 19th
142
NW Overton
NW Cornell
NW Lovejoy
NW Johnson
NW Westover
NW Hoyt
NW 17th
NW 14th
NW 12th
NW 10th
NW Flanders
I 405
NW Davis
NW 22nd
NW 21st
W Burnside
143
SW Oak
SW Vista
SW 20th
SW 18th
SW 16th
SW Washington
SW Morrison
SW 12th
SW 3rd
SW Jefferson
SW Salmon
161
SW Park
SW Broadway
Sunset Hwy
159
SW 5th
SW Hall
Washington Park
SW Montgomery
SW Laurel
SW Spring
SW Cardnell
SW 16th
147
SW Vista
SW Broadway
Naito Pkwy
SW Harbor
Broadw
Naito Pkwy
Fremont Bridge
River

1

Mi

Peaceniks & Civil Rights
North

NE Wygant

152

NE Prescott

N Commercial

N Vancouver

NE Grand

155

NE Rodney

NE Mason

NE 11th

162
150

NE Shaver

N Williams

NE Failing

NE 7th

NE 9th

NE Beech

NE Fremont

143

155

NE Ivy

NE Cook

149

N Gantenbein

NE Siskiyou

NE Morris

NE Rodney

NE Martin Luther King Jr

NE 12th

N Graham

N Russell

153

NE 9th

N Williams

NE Brazee

154

NE Sacramento

N Flint

I 5

NE Tillamook

NE Tillamook

NE San Rafael

N Wheeler

NE Hancock

st

0.5

NE Weidle

CHAPTER SIX

IDENTITIES & PROTESTS

1974–PRESENT

In 2002, protesters marched down SW Broadway Avenue to the Hilton Hotel where President George W. Bush was staying. When the Portland Police set up a roadblock, they went straight through it. *Bette Lee.*

O ne of the characters in the 2010 season of the TV series "Treme" (created by David Simon and Reedie Eric Overmyer) is Delmond Lambreaux. He is a jazz trumpet player, the New Orleans-born son of a traditional and proud "Mardi Gras Indian" Chief but now a New Yorker. In one scene, perhaps related to Overmyer's experience in Portland, Lambreaux's agent suggests the post-Katrina period is a good time to take advantage of his roots and proposes a concert tour starting in Portland, Oregon. Lambreaux (played by Rob Brown) makes fun of Portlanders by responding, "I've been in Portland. They're good people there but they clap on the one and three."

The reference reflects the new place that Portland occupies in the American cultural scene at the end of the first decade of the 21st century. The national media has focused on the city's draw for the young "creative class," its enterprising restaurants, and relatively affordable housing set in a celebrated natural environment. But the city's perhaps momentarily chic reputation seems to have dampened any surge in dissenting—let alone radical—activity after the spike of earlier decades.

Recent years have seen instead a significant shift in the ideology of dissent in America that has been reflected in Portland. The suppression of radical political movements during the Cold War and the McCarthy Era has been both the cause and the effect of the rise of identity politics—those movements for equality and justice for race, gender, sexual preference, and national or ethnic groups—as well as single issue politics devoted to separate issues such as peace, globalization, animal rights, and the environment. Some of these movements have radical roots. For gay rights, the 1948 **Progressive Party** 120 welcomed the support of "Bachelors for Wallace," organized by the Communist Harry Hay, which became the base for the early gay-rights group, the Mattachine Society. In 2009, a play based on Hay, "The Temperamentals" opened in New York.

CHAPTER SIX:
Identities & Protests

The current women's liberation movement developed from the experiences of women in New Left groups during the 1960s. But with the exception of a lively anarchist movement, most twenty-first century dissenters do not locate the source of their complaints within the nature of capitalism, so they do not consider a radical reorganization of society necessary to reach their goals. To the extent that they hope to achieve their objectives through reforms within capitalism, they distinguish themselves from previous radical history even if they practice or contemplate militant, confrontational, or even violent tactics. The strategy that guided most radical groups through much of the twentieth century—the organization of a popular political movement or party devoted to replacing capitalism with Socialism—has given way to the goal of reform through electoral and financial influence on the existing political structures of capitalism.

A compilation of forty-five street protests in Portland during the 1990s shows that the leading subjects were labor (including globalization) for seventeen, foreign policy for twelve, identity/civil rights for eight, and environment (mainly forest) for seven.[1] This fundamental fragmentation of dissenters into separate and often competing groups clearly has a negative impact on the prospects for movements for comprehensive radical change. Since the United States's defeat by the Vietnamese and the decline in the New Left, several institutions were established in Portland to provide these developing protest groups with a voice and alternatives to mainstream media—just like **Firebrand** 7 presented itself in 1895. These include the community radio station KBOO (1968–) and the progressive (now rarely) monthly *The Portland Alliance* (1981–). Michael Wells founded the counterculture *Portland Scribe* (1971–1979), which was once published at the **Centenary-Wilbur Methodist Church** 166, after its predecessor *Willamette Bridge* (1968–1971), expired. He later joined the less controversial "metrosexual" entertainment and cultural weekly, *Willamette Week*. The Red and Black Café at *400 SE 12th Avenue* makes radicals and protestors especially welcome. In 2010, it did not make a Portland police officer welcome after a series of controversial police killings of mentally ill people.

Protest movements have always been associated with their bookstores and the movements of this period were no exception. Bookstores serving activists have included The Days & Nights Bookstore on SW Broadway, across from Portland State University, operated by Jean-Paul

Pickens, an organizer for the Socialist Party's Young People's Socialist League; Radical Education Project's United Front Bookstore founded by Frank Giese; the Communist Party's **John Reed Bookstore 178** on SE Hawthorne Boulevard; and still hanging on in 2010, the collectively-run Laughing Horse Books at *12 NE 10th Avenue* just off E. Burnside Street (which mirrors the location of a better-known Powell's City of Books, at NW 10th Avenue and W. Burnside Street). The revived Wobblies and anarchists, who provide militancy and noisy energy at Portland demonstrations, recently had a bookstore in the basement of the Liberty Hall at *311 N. Ivy.*

Other activist institutions in Portland in the early twenty-first century include the **Centenary-Wilbur Methodist Church 166**, which hosted almost every organization of dissenters from the 1950s to 1980. Red Rose School provided movement-based education at the Friends Meeting House, *4312 SE Stark Street,* until it closed in 2002. Koinonia House, on the PSU campus at *633 SW Montgomery Street,* was a center for meetings, memorials, and services until it also closed. The Sisters of the Road Café at *133 NW 6th Avenue* was founded on the Catholic Worker Movement philosophy of Peter Maurin and Dorothy Day. The Pacific Green Party, originally a voice of the environmental movement, has contested some local elections and usually causes debate when third party candidates such as Ralph Nader, who drew fifty thousand votes in Oregon in the 2000 Presidential election, run under its banner. But the internet has probably become the most significant mode of communication and source of dissenting news on the Left. Widely available blogs and websites, such as the Portland Independent Media Center at portland.indymedia.org, are a growing alternative to mainstream media.

As this final section of the guide is devoted to more recent people and events—some of which readers may have witnessed or even participated in—the historical distance from the sites diminishes and their meaning may become more personal. So as some entries can be associated with personal memories rather than what we read or see in photos, documentary films, and videos, we become aware of the present as history. What we witness today is history tomorrow.

165 PORTLAND GAY LIBERATION FRONT 🎙

Less than a year after the Stonewall Rebellion of New York gays, the **Portland Gay Liberation Front** was organized on March 10, 1970, at the

The Harbor Club was Portland's preeminent gay bar until city officials forced it to close in 1965. Its marquis can be seen on the far right side of this photo. *Oregon Historical Society, OrHi52847.*

Centenary-Wilbur Methodist Church 166 by Holly Hart and Jack Wilkinson, who were both twenty-two years old.[2] Five years earlier, the city had forced Portland's premier gay bar since the 1940s, The Harbor Club at 65 *SW Yamhill Street* (now Paddy's Bar and Grill), to close.[3] The balcony where much of the action reportedly took place in the old days is still visible from the back room. Frank Ivancie, the last of Portland's old-line mayors, who held office from 1980–1984, led the resistance to gays and lesbians in city government. "No homos in fire houses," was one of his more notorious declarations.

166 CENTENARY-WILBUR METHODIST CHURCH 🌐

Recalling the record of the **Methodist Federation for Social Action 133** in the 1950s and 1960s, is there something about the Methodist church in Portland that recommends it to radicals? Indeed, as early as the 1950s the Federation already had sponsored a talk by then GOP Senator Wayne Morse in the **Centenary-Wilbur Methodist Church** at *215 SE 9th Avenue*. By 1970, the church had been transformed from a prosperous middle-class institution reflecting its early neighborhood demographics of the nineteenth century to the end of World War II into a counterculture center that served Portland dissidents and hippies. The historic church itself never recovered from damage caused by the Columbus Day storm of 1962, but its education building survived. Until the church's demise in 1980, it welcomed dissident groups ranging from the Gay Liberation Front and the People's Liberation Army to the New American Movement, the Poor People's Alliance, and the Trojan Decommissioning Alliance, bringing down surveillance by the Portland **Red Squad 194**.[4] Many Portlanders associate the church with the site's later tenants, the music venue La Luna and the Pine Street Theater. In 2006, the building was remodeled into the Pine Street Lofts.

167 CITY CLUB OF PORTLAND

Although its male members rejected women in three consecutive elections, the **City Club of Portland**, which usually holds its meeting in the Governor Hotel at *614 SW 11th Avenue*, finally accepted them in 1973 with a 65 percent majority vote. The Multnomah Club also allowed women to vote in the 1970s. They were still well ahead of the other men-only clubs that dominated Portland's business and political life during the twentieth century. The University Club did not admit women until 1990 and the Arlington Club, whose members meet at *811 SW Salmon Street*, hung on until 1991. During the struggle over women at the Arlington in 1990, *The Oregonian*, published by Arlington Club member Fred Stickel, killed a story reporting the Club's efforts to delay a vote on a city ordinance that would require them to let women into the Club.[5]

168 JIM HILL: "WE ARE PORTLAND TOO!"

Jim Hill, a former railroad gandy dancer and longshoreman, came to Portland's Skid Road a year after the 1971–2 strike. For twenty-one years, he worked on the docks as a member of Longview Local 21 of the International Longshore and Warehouse Union, but his union brothers finally had to refer him to an alcoholism treatment program. By 1974, **Julia Ruuttila 175** called him the "Bard of Burnside" when he began writing poetry while working for the former Transit Bank at *18 NW 3rd Avenue*.

But the only book he ever published turned out to be defiantly titled, *We Are Portland Too!* The slim jumble of typed and printed pages was briefly offered in the late 1970s through the old Green Dolphin bookstore at *215 SW Ankeney*.

Hill should be read in the company of Portland worker poets who include Herman Eich (**Firebrand 7**), Paddy Flynn, and "Dublin Dan" Liston, whose poetry appears in the 1934 longshore strikers' mimeographed bulletin *The Hook*.

The voice in Hill's title poem demands that attention must be paid to his class and place. Like the poetry of other worker poets, it's not

CHAPTER SIX: Identities & Protests

the product of a schooled member of the poet's profession, but it's still worth our time.

We Are Portland Too!

Though we're older
and weathered with time
And most of our buildings
covered with ages of grime
We will not be hidden
from the minds of men
This is where the heritage
Of Oregon began,
The early-day logger,
The waterfront scene
The coming of the railroad
And stout-hearted men,
And Burnside was hacked out
of the towering green
And this is where the city
Of Portland began.
As you look down
from your lofty heights
At tall gleaming towers
and wonderful sights
Remember us yet
when passing through...
We are Portland, too!

Doug Spangle, another local poet, was impressed by Hill:

Laureate

Below the White Stag's
night light neon
down on Second Street

old Jim Hill,
Skid Road's poet,
stoops to the spat-on sidewalk
and picks up a yellow, green
and orange leaf with a look
so gentle, so…
I rush past,
 pretending not to look.

169 PORTLAND LABOR COLLEGE, LABOR EDUCATION 🌐

The second coming of the **Portland Labor College** (see also site 44) occurred in 1977, when several unions and other sponsors, led by the former International Woodworkers of America (IWA), opened a center for labor education under the direction of Norman Diamond. Before closing in 1984, the college, located in the former Operating Engineers Union Hall on SW 2nd Avenue, also sponsored a theater troupe that revived the former name of the Portland Labor Players, which performed plays about working class struggle, such as *Season of Silence: Life and Labor in the Oregon City Woolen Mills*, a play about the 1907 strike at the Mills. Plays were outdoors at **International Longshore and Warehouse Union's (ILWU) Bloody Thursday 57** observances in Oaks Park and all around town at, for

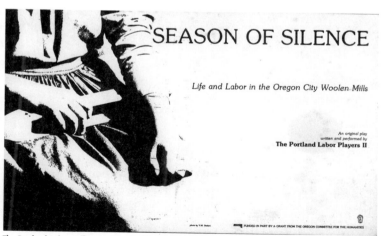

SEASON OF SILENCE

Life and Labor in the Oregon City Woolen Mills

An original play
written and performed by
The Portland Labor Players II

photo by T.M. Stetson ▪ FUNDED IN PART BY A GRANT FROM THE OREGON COMMITTEE FOR THE HUMANITIES

The Portland Labor College and Portland Labor Players II made a brief comeback in the late 1970s. They performed the play *Season of Silence*, depicting historic attacks on Chinese workers. *Norman Diamond.*

CHAPTER SIX:
Identities & Protests

example, the Musicians Union Hall at *325 NE 20th Avenue*, St. Johns YMCA, at *8010 N. Charleston Avenue*, and the Theater Workshop, at *511 SE 60th Avenue*.

170 BILL WALTON 🌳

Bill Walton, counterculture center for the NBA Champion Portland Trail Blazers in 1977, shared a November 5 birthday with Eugene Debs and lived at *2337 NW Kearney Street*. The police **Red Squad 194** accused him of joining anti-Vietnam War protests while in college and, in Portland, of associating with radicals, including Jack Scott, a sports journalist working to develop political consciences of professional athletes. Walton visited his old place twenty years later and noted "it hadn't changed at all"—although the rent, then sixty-five dollars a month, surely had.

Bill Walton was the Portland Trail Blazers' counter-culture center in the late 1970s. He was accused by the Red Squad of joining anti-Vietnam protests and associating with radicals in Portland. *Oregon Historical Society, OrHi82630.*

171 FRANCIS J. MURNANE WHARF

Portland's **Francis J. Murnane Wharf** (destroyed in 2009) at the seawall at the foot of *SW Ankeny Street* was the only public memorial to a union leader in the state of Oregon, a fact that testifies to the pro-business, anti-labor bias of official history. The floating dock, dedicated by **ILWU 57** President Harry Bridges in 1979, was destroyed in 2009, an act that can only be described as "city-sponsored vandalism." It honored the late leader of the Congress of Industrial Organization's (CIO) International Woodworkers of America and later of ILWU Local 8 who died in 1968 while conducting a union meeting. During the McCarthy Era, Murnane defended radicals as secretary of the Julia Eaton Ruuttila Defense Committee in 1948 and, as head of the Harry Bridges Defense Committee in 1949, he denounced the **Red Squad 194** for making Bridges a special target. He was also a **Progressive Party 120** candidate for the state legislature in 1948 and in his later years became leader of historic preservation efforts in Portland. Murnane believed that radicals "[Eugene] Debs and [Bill] Haywood showed the way" for unions. Bridges noted at the dedication that Murnane always hoped "that the old slogan of the Wobblies would come true: 'Workers of the World Unite.'" Father Bertram Griffin of St. Andrews Catholic Church blessed the wharf for the use of "radicals, labor activists, and lovers." Among the major supporters of the memorial were **Julia Ruuttila 175** and fellow ILWU Local 40 leader, the late **Jesse Stranahan 174.**[6]

Francis J. Murnane led the ILWU and defended radicals his entire life. The wharf named after him was located on the west bank of the Willamette River, at the foot of SW Ankeny Street. *Colin Smith.*

172 RICHARD ROSS

Although McCarthyism was considered by many to be dead, its hidden secrets continue to be revealed. Longtime Portland KGW-TV news anchor **Richard Ross** (later at KATU) waited until 1977 to confess he had been an FBI informer in the 1950s, reporting on the politics of his

CHAPTER SIX:
Identities & Protests

colleagues in Portland's TV, radio, and print journalism. Ross retired from KATU in 1986 and took a public relations job promoting the Oregon Lottery.

173 STEW ALBERT 🌳

Portlander **Stew Albert** (1939–2006) was one of the "leaders" of the

yippies in the 1960s, and an unindicted co-conspirator of the "Chicago 7" defendants whose convictions for organizing violence at the 1968 Democratic convention in Chicago were reversed on appeal. In 1985, he moved to Portland where he remained an activist and produced his popular website. One of his local political observations was that most speakers at Portland antiwar demonstrations were boring, and he argued for adoption of yippie tactics such as spontaneous self-expression and a fun spirit to liven them up. He is buried in the Havurah Shalom Cemetery, *5656 SW Humphrey Boulevard.*

Stew Albert, longtime radical activist, moved to Portland in 1985. This photo shows him in Berkeley, California, at a rally in 1969. Robert Altman.

174 JESSE & LOIS STRANAHAN 🌳

Jesse and Lois Stranahan were active in almost every local political and labor struggle from the time they met at Commonwealth College in Mena, Arkansas, in the late 1930s. Jesse was a journalist on the CIO's newspaper, *Labor New Dealer,* and a leader in the ILWU's Clerks Local 40. Lois remains an activist in labor politics. One of her arrests, for gathering petition signatures against the sales tax at the Fred Meyer store at *SE 82nd Avenue and Foster Road,* occurred in 1988. Years later, a jury awarded her more than $2 million for the false arrest, but the Oregon Supreme Court reversed that decision.

175 JULIA RUUTTILA 🌳

Julia Ruuttila (1907–1991)—also known by her maiden name Godman, previous married names Bertram and Eaton, and pen names Kathleen

Cronin and Kathleen Ruuttila—was prominent among the Old Left radicals for whom age alone put an end to their activism.[7] In her lifetime, there were few labor or civil liberties struggles in which Ruuttila did not participate, especially those conducted by the CIO Woodworkers and ILWU unions. She was both victim and militant opponent of McCarthyism. She participated in anti-Vietnam War protests, fought against Oregon nerve gas storage and the sales tax, and worked for public power. In the 1930s, she organized the effort to free the last of the **Centralia Wobblies 39**, and in 1948 she provided help for the **Vanport Flood victims 115**. Ruuttila was fired by the Oregon Public Welfare Commission for her support of the Vanport refugees after S. Eugene Allen, editor of the *Oregon Labor Press*, denounced her as "another energetic little lady who promotes the Communist Party line." In turn, Ruuttila described Allen as "the most vicious right wing." Frequently depicted in the press as a dissenter, Ruuttila, then sixty-six, together with **Martina Gangle Curl 178**, who was sixty-eight, was jailed in 1973 for refusing to leave Portland General Electric offices at *SW Broadway and Morrison Street*

Julia Ruuttila was one of Portland's most prominent and involved radical activists. There were few labor or civil liberties struggles that she didn't participate in. She's shown here, being arrested in 1966. *Oregon Historical Society, OrHi23920.*

to protest rising electricity rates. In one of her poems, she counted the carriage rings in Northwest Portland curbs and found more on affluent blocks than poor ones. "Carriage rings," her poem concludes, "defined the social status/In old Portland."

176 DON CHAMBERS ♀

> Old revolutionaries are the gentle dignity of a city.
> — Rick Rubin on Don Chambers, 1985

The Oregon Supreme Court upheld the two-year suspension of attorney **Don Chambers** in 1982, although, because he was almost blind and unable to walk, he had already retired a year earlier. Chambers, of an anarchist bent, was called "the most radical lawyer in Portland" for his defense, with fees, of "the poor, the Communists, Trotskyites, Chicanos, Native Americans, and prostitutes" as well as motorcycle gang members and students arrested in the **1970 Battle of the Park Blocks 159**. With a tiny office next to his Check Store locker service on *NW 2nd Avenue and Burnside Street*, Chambers was the subject of many complaints from more elevated members of the Bar, although the revival of a local chapter of the National Lawyers Guild made defense of unpopular causes more respectable.

177 BENJAMIN LINDER ♀

Benjamin Linder (1959–1987) is commemorated with a bench ("a bench against forgetting," his sister called it) and a tree in Wallace Park at *NW 25th Avenue and Raleigh Street*, near his former home, where four hundred people marked the tenth anniversary of his death.[8] There is also a large multi-wall mural in his honor near the bookstore in Reed College's Gray Student Center. Linder was assassinated by U.S.-state-sponsored terrorists in 1987 while building water projects in Nicaragua for the benefit of poor rural residents. A professional clown and engineering graduate of the University of Washington, Linder volunteered his services to the Sandinista government, which the Reagan administration sought to overthrow by funding the counter-revolutionary Contras. He is also remembered by the Ben Linder Construction Brigade. The seventh contingent of its volunteers went to Corinto, Nicaragua (one of Portland's sister cities), in 1996 to work on local projects in Linder's honor.

One Linder Brigade member was the late **Dr. David Hanson "Punch" Worthington** (1935–2006), a long-time labor, peace, and health activist from Keizer, Oregon. His family asked that "Punch would be best honored if well-wishers voted for leaders who will defend our bill of rights, preserve our wilderness, fight for socialized health care, and protect the rights of labor unions in the U.S. and abroad."

178 HANK & MARTINA GANGLE CURL 🌐

Veteran Communist Party members **Hank and Martina Gangle Curl** were among the proprietors of the John Reed Bookstore at *4700 SE Hawthorne Boulevard* and offered Portlanders leftist books and literature until it closed in 1993. Martina (1906–1994) was a prominent artist and Hank was a skilled ships' carpenter.

Hank Curl (1913–2010) died at Bay City, where as long he could, he helped out at the Museum of People's Art, which championed Martina's work as well as other radical Northwest artists. He had moved there from their home at *2237 NE Clackamas Street*, which has been occupied by important Portland artists for many years. It was originally owned by Harry Wentz, dean of the Portland Museum Art School, and later by his friends, the outstanding Northwest radical painters, brothers Arthur and Albert Runquist. Their Works Progress Administration (WPA) murals can be seen

Martina Gangle Curl was photographed with the leader of the Red Squad, John Keegan, on July 15, 1941, in an attempt to paint her as a traitor to the labor movement. *City of Portland Archives, A2001-074.22.*

at the University of Oregon Library, Pendleton High School, and the Sedro Wooley, Washington, Post Office. Martina Curl's Rose City Park School mural at *2334 NE 57th Avenue* features the early white migration to Oregon. Efforts to save her artwork if the school is closed have been planned.

179 PETE SEEGER 🌳

In 1994, radical folksinger Pete Seeger's last Portland concert—a benefit for the Northwest Tree Planters and Farm Workers United (PCUN)—was held at Benson High School at *546 NE 12th Avenue*. In 1955, students made a bootleg recording of his concert at Reed College, which Reed President Frank L. Griffin originally opposed but finally agreed to it if there was no outside publicity. Seeger immediately demanded the students stop selling the ten-inch double LP set.

180 CELEBRATION OF JOHN REED'S BIRTH

On October 22, 1987, Pioneer Square was the scene of a celebration of John Reed's birth. A small group of local writers, including David Milholland, the late Fred DeWolfe, Brian Booth, Walt Curtis, and David Horowitz, with financial support from Reed fan Corliss Lamont in New York, held an appreciative reading of Reed's writing. The organizers later established the Oregon Cultural Heritage Commission, which installed the **Reed Memorial Bench in Washington Park** 31.

181 MAY DAY IN PORTLAND

May Day observances in Portland have been revived in recent years with marches downtown supported by a few unions and younger radicals. The police attack on demonstrators in 2001 exposed the role of rightist police and the **Red Squad** 194. Black clad anarchists lent energy to the marches up Broadway and downtown with drum corps, while cheerleaders roused spirits with well-coordinated protest yells.

182 PORTLAND'S HALLS 🌳

In the 1990s **Finnish Hall** was moved from its original location at *3425 N. Montana Avenue* and remodeled into a Community Center for Kaiser Permanente's N. Interstate Avenue complex. It was one of the old Portland ethnic and nationality halls that radicals seemed to favor for their meetings and social gatherings since early in the twentieth century. In addition to Finnish Hall were **Norse Hall** at *111 NE 11th Avenue*, **Linnea Hall** at *2066 NW Irving Street*, **Italian Federation Hall** at *SW 4th Avenue and Madison Street*, **Swiss Hall** at *SW 3rd Avenue and*

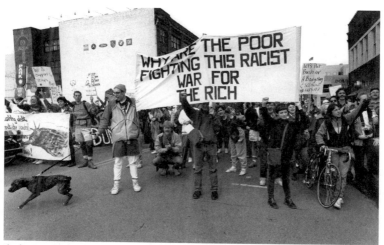

The first President Bush was surprised by the number of protestors— fifteen thousand —that marched up Broadway on January 12, 1991, against the invasion of Iraq. *Bette Lee.*

Jefferson Street, **Hibernian Hall** on *NE Russell Street*, and **Turn Verein Hall**, which stood at *SW 4th Avenue and Yamhill Street.*

183 THE WHITE PANTHERS
The White Panthers were another radical group inspired by the Black Panther Party and were first organized in Michigan. The Portland White Panthers were accused of throwing a Molotov cocktail through the window of draft ("Selective Service") headquarters in August, 1970. In December, the FBI and Portland Police raided the group's house at 3436 SW 1st Avenue. Two White Panthers were arrested. Two months later, their leader, Bob Yaple, was convicted by a federal jury in Portland for possession of bomb-making materials and sentenced to prison.

184 LITTLE BEIRUT
The story of how Portland achieved the national nickname of **Little Beirut** has been traced to former **President George H. W. Bush**, who denied coining the name. After several smaller demonstrations against him, Bush was evidently shocked when fifteen thousand marched up Broadway on January 12, 1991, in the first major demonstration against his imminent invasion of Iraq.

His son **George W. Bush** also has not been warmly received in Portland. In 2002, police rioted with tear gas and rubber bullets against thousands of

President George H. W. Bush made Portland famous by declaring it "Little Beirut" in 1991. *Bette Lee.*

demonstrators while Bush was raising money for Oregon Republican Senator Gordon Smith at the Hilton Hotel downtown. The next year, five thousand protested another Bush fundraiser at the University of Portland. During the 2004 election campaign, Bush avoided the city, retreating to the suburbs with an indoor event in Beaverton, while Democrat John Kerry drew fifty thousand to a rally at *Waterfront Park*.

185 BILL AND HELEN GORDON & THE JEWISH COMMUNITY CENTER 🌐

In 1995, **Bill Gordon** (1908–2009) received the first Gladys McCoy Volunteer Award from retired **Judge Mercedes Deiz 140** on behalf of Multnomah County. Bill and his wife, **Helen** (1912–1984), arrived in Portland in 1953 to work at the **Jewish Community Center** at *1636 SW 13th Avenue*. That center, which was destroyed by "urban renewal" in 1971, was renamed the Mittleman Jewish Community Center and moved to the Southwest suburbs. In 1914, the center had been established because "other clubs would not allow Jews to become members."9 The Gordons were active in peace and civil rights actions and later in the Gray Panthers, and Judge Deiz especially remembered them for "all kinds of civil rights activities for things Oregon so badly needed." When Bill was ninety, Portland folkies Kate Power and Steve Einhorn played at a concert with **Pete Seeger 179**, who considered Bill and Helen to be close friends. Pete told them he appreciated Helen's "gently savvy gift for swaying politicians" toward social change. Her style was "just perfect," Pete said. A plaque at PSU honors Helen with these words: "Because of her love for children and her energy in their behalf, Oregon is a richer community."

186 FERN GAGE 🌳

In 1996, the children of **Fern Gage**, a Portland peace activist since 1945, donated her library to the organization in which she was most active, the **Fellowship of Reconciliation 102** at *6437 SW Virginia Avenue*. Gage, who began working in church and civil rights groups, was also a supporter of the **Women's International League for Peace and Freedom (WILPF) 29**. Evelyn Murray (1911–1996), another Portland WILPF member, was especially active in the campaign against chemical warfare in the 1970s.

187 ACE HAYES

Portland's leading muckraking journalist, **Ace Hayes**, published his Free Press and held monthly "Secret Government" seminars at The Clinton Street Theater at *2522 SE Clinton Street* until his death in 1998. His

encyclopedic knowledge of government scandal and cover-ups attracted some conspiracy theorists, but his own 1993 investigation uncovered corrupt Portland **Red Squad 194** activities, such as its link to the Anti-Defamation League of the Jewish community and the FBI.

Ace Hayes was Portland's leading muckraking journalist. He published *Free Press,* held monthly "Secret Government" meetings, and investigated the Red Squad until his death in 1998. *City of Portland Archives, A2004-005.*

188 ISAKA SHAMSUD-DIN

Isaka Shamsud-Din (born Isaac Allen, 1941–) arrived in Portland in 1947 with his parents and nine siblings from rural east Texas, and lived in

Vanport until it washed away in the flood the next year. As a Portland State College (now University) art student in 1965, he won a competition to paint a fifteen-foot high mural in the south stairway between the second and third floors for the new Smith Memorial Student Center on *1825 SW Broadway*. Although there is only one specific reference to the former city (the address: "290 Broadacres"), he called his mural "Vanport." Shamsud-Din's vision, however, was informed not only by his personal memories, but by research from which he concluded that the failure of the authorities to warn residents of the flood danger was "an official effort to disperse black folks."

As he told art critic Randy Gragg in 1998, the dead man being lifted in the lower left of the mural was the black activist John Daniels, a teacher who committed suicide. Shamsud-Din painted his body with an African-motif scarf as a symbol of respect and honor. Daniels was a class president at PSU and previously senior class president of the last class to graduate from the former Lincoln High School in 1952—now Lincoln Hall at PSU.

After painting the mural, Shamsud-Din dropped out of college and joined the Student Nonviolent Coordinating Committee in Arkansas. In 1968, he joined the Nation of Islam and adopted his present name. He later returned to Portland and was active in the mural movement,

The Sylvania campus of Portland Community College is home to this mural of Northwest Labor history. Designed by faculty member Bill Garnett and painted by his students, the mural shows familiar faces and places of the struggle. *Colin Smith.*

including completing one at the Cleve Allen Dental Clinic at *213 N. Russell Street,* originally established by the Black Panthers as the **Malcolm X Dental Clinic 154**, The artist returned to PSU for his BA and MA degrees in art. Shamsud-Din has had several Portland exhibits and maintains an online studio at www.isakashamsuddin.com.

189 PORTLAND COMMUNITY COLLEGE'S "REMEMBER"

A Northwest labor history mural, **"Remember,"** was dedicated at Portland Community College's Sylvania Campus in 1999. Sponsored by campus unions, designed by art faculty member Bill Garnett, and painted by his students, the mural depicts, among others, **Dr. Marie Equi 16, Julia Ruuttila 175,** the early Wobbly martyrs, as well as today's Northwest Tree Planters and Farm Worker's United (PCUN), and Jobs with Justice.

190 WOODY GUTHRIE CIRCLE

Woody Guthrie, world-famous composer of our national folk anthem, "This Land is Your Land," is one of the few radicals officially honored in Portland (also see site 91). However, he is not honored by the City of Portland, but rather stealthily by the federal government's Bonneville Power Administration (BPA). In 2001, with almost no publicity, the administration named the driveway at its headquarters **"Woody Guthrie Circle"** and erected three stones inscribed with verses from his songs "Roll on Columbia" and "Pastures of Plenty." A large tapestry of Guthrie also hangs in the lobby of the BPA building at 905 NE 11th Avenue, and the film for which Woody wrote his music is available from the BPA Library. Much of the credit for the memorial goes to two former BPA employees: folk singer Bill Murlin and the late **Elmer Buehler 92.**

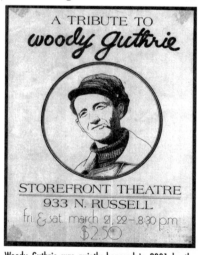

Woody Guthrie was quietly honored in 2001 by the Bonneville Power Administration when they named the driveway at its headquarters "Woody Guthrie Circle." This poster comes from a much louder tribute to Guthrie held at the Storefront Theater in 1975. *Barbara Davis.*

In contrast, a year before the 2001 dedication of the Portland memorial, Guthrie's name was removed from the BPA's substation in Hood River when ownership was transferred to the Hood River Electric Co-op. Hood River's anti-Communist business leaders, who also removed Japanese American names from the town's honor roll during World War II, objected to the original designation in 1990. In 2000, they pressured the Co-op board to rename it for Willard Johnson, its first manager. They acted with unintentional irony, having forgotten that Johnson himself had strongly supported the Guthrie name against the local opposition, declaring that the "world would be better off with a few more Woody Guthries in it."

191 ANARCHIST CONVENTION 1993 🌐

"The Great Anarchist Riot" was the tongue-in-cheek label applied to the **1993 Anarchist Convention** outside the former X-Ray Café at *SW 3rd and Burnside Street*. Casualties included broken windows, bruises, and national media attention.

192 KENDRA JAMES

Kendra James (1982–2003) was one of too many Portlanders killed by Portland police during the first decade of the twenty-first century. Police officer Scott McCollister shot her after a traffic stop when he claimed to have been endangered when she tried to drive away. In most cases of police shootings, the victims were black and usually not confronted for a violent act. In the James case, as well as others, community uproar erupted in the wake of the shooting and city officials promised reforms in police procedures and denied profiling and other racist practices. A more recent case was that of Keaton Otis, killed by police in May, 2010.

193 THE CIA & SCOTT D. CAPLAN 🌐

Scott D. Caplan, of the law firm of Jordan, Caplan, Paul, and Etter, fronted for a phony CIA cutout company, "Bayard Foreign Marketing, LLC" headed by a fictitious "Leonard Thomas Bayard," which in 2004 was exposed as a key component of the Bush administration's "extraordinary rendition" program. Caplan's firm's offices in suite 755 of the Pittock Block, *921 SW Washington Street,* were used to buy and register the civilian jet the CIA used most often to kidnap suspected terrorists and fly them to be tortured in cooperating countries or in the CIA's own secret prisons. Portland Peaceful Response Coalition held a protest at the offices in September 2005. In 2007, the Oregon State Bar, when asked to consider whether Caplan had violated the Bar's ethics by setting up a false Oregon corporation, dismissed the complaint on the basis that "a law" prohibits Caplan from revealing information about a client who did not exist. The Bar's Mary Cooper declined to cite that "law," which probably was the notorious "state secrets" claim made to hide CIA activities from the public.

An earlier CIA contact in Portland (1949–1950), to whom prospective job seekers and information peddlers were referred, was a Mr. J. S. Bailey, with an office in room 414 of the Lewis Building downtown.

194 THE PORTLAND POLICE RED SQUAD 🌳

The Red Squad of the Portland Police Bureau has been a notorious presence in Portland since before the World War I Red Scare. But because it still constitutes the city's political police as the Bureau's Criminal Intelligence Unit and operates from the tenth floor of police headquarters at *1111 SW 2nd Avenue*, its site is placed at the most contemporary chronological place in this guide—the end. In recent years, its surveillance and reporting have been focused on anarchist groups and antiwar, May Day, and environmental protests.

Until 2005, the city ordered two of its Red Squad members to join the FBI in Portland's Joint Anti-Terrorism Task Force (JTTF). That was the year the city council voted to make Portland the first city in the nation to condition continued assignment of its police officers on the FBI's granting of full oversight on their activities to the mayor and the chief of police. The FBI refused and the two officers were withdrawn. A Portland activist, Red Emma, wrote JTTF's secret theme song to the tune of "Every Breath You Take" by The Police. It begins:

> Every breath you take
> Every move you make
> Evidence we'll fake of the laws you break —
> We'll be watching you

Throughout its long history, the Red Squad has drawn most of its members from the ranks of ideologically extreme right-wing officers. In the

CHAPTER SIX:
Identities & Protests

1930s, when the Red Squad had its office in room 428 of what is now the Oregon Pioneer Building at *SW Stark Street and 3rd Avenue* (then called the Railway Exchange Building), it functioned as an outspoken right-wing political gang funded with public and private funds. According to a scathing report by Gus Solomon and several other leading attorneys, the Red Squad spent its money on infiltrating and spying on labor and political organizations, organizing raids and provocations, and engaging in violent strike suppression. It even operated a clearinghouse for employers to blacklist leftists as potential employees. The Red Squad's leader was the right-wing ideologue Walter B. Odale, a Portland police patrolman whose claimed rank of captain was actually in the U.S. Army Reserve. He supervised dangerous provocateurs like George Marion Stroup, who was never a sworn police officer but an American Legion anti-subversive activities agent, the violent provocateur Hal Marchant, and former bootlegger Merriel R. Bacon, who masqueraded as a Communist Party member.[10] During the McCarthy Era, the Red Squad was headed by another extremist, Detective William D. Browne, once the only member of the American Legion's "Americanization" Committee.

A warning to the Mayor from the head of the Red Squad:

CONFIDENTIAL
Portland, Jan. 6, 1949
To: Mayor [Dorothy] Lee
Chief of Police
FBI
File
A group of Communists and sympathizers are attempting to promote a movement among the colored people of the city to bring "Mass Pressure" to bear on the new Mayor's administration to force passage of what they call a Civil Rights Ordinance which would require hotels, restaurants and theaters and other places of business which serve the public to cater to colored people on the same basis as to whites and to make it unlawful for them to refuse to do so.
—W. B. Odale, Captain, Portland Police Bureau

This photo demonstrates the extent to which the city was intent on keeping track of organized labor and Communist activity. The back of the photo reads: "Chief Niles — This photo was taken Wed, April 10, 1935. It shows the Communist gathering in the Plaza. I am keeping a photographic record of the 'Red' activities in Portland and will gladly supply the 'RED SQUAD' with copies on request. Paul Callicote." *Portland City Archives, A2001-074.80.*

Against all evidence, every mayor—from Joe Carson in the early 1930s to Vera Katz in 2004—has denied the Red Squad's existence, although sometimes they only stonewalled by saying that the police bureau's table of organization did not include a "Red Squad." Such false denials were frequently exposed when the Red Squad's routinely unlawful behavior was uncovered in the press or in other investigations. In 1996, a Multnomah County court found that undercover Red Squad spy Larry Siewert, who was assigned to track radicals and subversives, violated a Portlander's civil rights. Siewert actually spied and reported on the lawful activities of a wide range of peace, environmental, and equal rights organizations. He later became Mayor Katz's personal bodyguard.

In 2002, the Red Squad was confronted with yet another scandal when the Portland Tribune revealed that officer Winfield Falk, a member of the extremist John Birch Society and Red Squad member, had stolen Red Squad files from the early 1960s through the 1980s. The courts previously had ordered that the records be destroyed. Falk had hidden them on his property, intending to send them to his ideological comrades in private Red hunting groups in the east. After his death, the files were found and excerpts published in the *Portland Tribune*, which eventually deposited them in the Portland City Archives. Those files even included surveillance of future Mayor Vera Katz who, in her younger

CHAPTER SIX: Identities & Protests

activist days, supported a farm workers grape boycott. Ironically, once in office, Katz became a devoted defender of the Red Squad against its critics until she left office in 2004.

1974 – PRESENT NOTES

1. "Ten years of Portland activism," *The Portland Alliance,* December, 1999.

2. *The Oregonian,* March 16, 2004.

3. For a historical account of the **GLT** identities movement, see *A Walking Tour of Downtown Portland: A Century of Gay, Lesbian, and Transgender Historical Sites* (1999), published by the Gay and Lesbian Archives of the Pacific Northwest and stored at the Oregon Historical Society.

4. David Kohl, "Portland's Centenary-Wilbur Methodist Church: Probably the City's Most Significant Venue for Social Change in the 1960s – 1970s." Unpublished Manuscript, 2005.

5. "Portland 1974–1999," *Willamette Week,* November 10, 1999.

6. *The Dispatcher,* October 5, 1979.

7. Sandy Polishuk, *Sticking to the Union: An Oral History of the Life and Times of Julia Ruuttila* (New York: Palgrave Macmillan, 2003).

8. Joan Kruckewitt, *The Death of Ben Linder: The Story of a North American in Sandinista Nicaragua* (New York: Seven Stories Press, 2000).

9. *Portland Tribune,* August 30, 2006.

10. Thomas S. Wilson, Alan Hart, Harlow F. Lenon, Chris Boesen, H. M. Esterly, and Gus Solomon, "Report of the Civil Liberties Committee" (National Lawyers Guild, Oregon Chapter, May 24, 1938).

Identities
& Protests

Identities & Protests
Westside

A FINAL WORD

Francis J. Murnane led the annual Bloody Thursday commemoration march for years as the head of the ILWU. This photo was taken of a July 5, 1967, march as the union moved east along SW 3rd Avenue. *Oregon Historical Society, OrHi101729.*

I f you've come this far in *The Portland Red Guide*, it may be that you were interested, stimulated, amused, or maybe even angered enough by the alternate history it presents to see it through. If so, you are probably aware that it is hardly the last word on this large and controversial subject. Indeed, one reason it required more than a decade from inception to publication is that it never seemed—and indeed it still doesn't seem—to be done. New sites were constantly suggested to me by people, daily newspapers, and books. They all demanded investigation, so I was faced with a constant worry that someone or something important was going to be left out.

So apologies are due in advance for being unaware, for forgetting, or for overlooking both obvious and obscure sites that evoke Portland's radical past. Readers to whom those apologies are appropriate are invited to set the record straight by communicating with me via Ooligan Press—both to educate me and, possibly, to justify an expanded edition in the future. Especially invited are corrections of or additions to the listings and narratives.

But for now, please regard *The Portland Red Guide* in your hands as a modest start toward a more respectful public understanding and rehabilitation of a neglected part of Portland's common heritage.

WALKING TOURS

WALKING TOUR ONE: INNER NORTHWEST AND BURNSIDE STREET
TOTAL SITES: 8
TOTAL DISTANCE: 0.25 MILES

STARTING POINT

130 DISPATCH OFFICE OF THE MARINE COOKS & STEWARDS BRANCH (LEFTIST UNION)
127 West Burnside Street

FIRST STOP

176 DON CHAMBER'S OFFICE
NW 2nd Avenue and West Burnside Street
Directions: Walk west on Burnside less than half a block to NW 2nd Avenue.
Miles: 0.03

SECOND STOP

11 ERICKSON'S SALOON (CURRENTLY BARRACUDA NIGHTCLUB)
9 NW 2nd Avenue
Directions: Take a right at NW 2nd Avenue. Your destination is a half block up on the left.
Miles: 0.02

THIRD STOP

94 OREGON NIKKEI LEGACY CENTER
121 NW 2nd Avenue
Directions: Continue walking up NW 2nd Avenue. Your destination is a half block past Couch on the left.
Miles: 0.05

FOURTH STOP

59 THE MARINE WORKERS INDUSTRIAL UNION
219 NW Davis Street
Directions: Continue up NW 2nd Avenue to Davis and take a left. Your destination is on the right.
Miles: 0.04

FIFTH STOP

94 OSHU NIPPO OFFICES IN THE MERCHANT HOTEL (CURRENTLY OLD TOWN PIZZA)
226 NW Davis Street
Directions: This destination is across the street from the previous destination.
Miles: 0

SIXTH STOP

59 VILLA ROOMS (CURRENTLY UNION GOSPEL MISSION)
9 NW 3rd Avenue
Directions: Continue west on Davis and take a left at 3rd Avenue. Continue up 3rd past Couch Street; your destination will be on the right.
Miles: 0.1

LAST STOP

6 THE FIFTH REGIMENT OF COXEY'S ARMY
SW 3ʀᴅ Aᴠᴇɴᴜᴇ ᴀɴᴅ Wᴇꜱᴛ Bᴜʀɴꜱɪᴅᴇ Sᴛʀᴇᴇᴛ

Directions: Continue walking south on NW 3rd Avenue to the corner of 3rd and
Burnside.

Mɪʟᴇꜱ: 0.01

To get back to your starting point, walk east on Burnside Street for one-and-a-half blocks. To continue
your Northwest Portland tour, walk north on Burnside to Everett (0.2 miles) and take a left. Then,
begin the directions for Walking Tour Two.

WALKING TOUR TWO: NORTHWEST AND BURNSIDE STREET
TOTAL SITES: 5
TOTAL DISTANCE: 0.77 MILES

STARTING POINT

10 REV. SHEPARD S. FREEMAN'S HOME
314 NW Eᴠᴇʀᴇᴛᴛ Sᴛʀᴇᴇᴛ

FIRST STOP

17 IWW MEETING HALL (CURRENTLY CONDOMINIUMS)
535 NW Dᴀᴠɪꜱ Sᴛʀᴇᴇᴛ

Directions: Walk west on Everett to NW 5th Avenue and take a left. Walk one
block to Davis and take a right. You will find your destination on the right.

Mɪʟᴇꜱ: 0.2

SECOND STOP

69 DR. DENORVAL UNTHANK'S OFFICE
SW 6ᴛʜ Aᴠᴇɴᴜᴇ ᴀɴᴅ Wᴇꜱᴛ Bᴜʀɴꜱɪᴅᴇ Sᴛʀᴇᴇᴛ

Directions: Continue west on Davis Street to 6th Avenue and take a left. Walk
up 6th Avenue to Burnside Street.

Mɪʟᴇꜱ: 0.1

THIRD STOP

10 BETHEL AFRICAN EPISCOPAL CHURCH
226 NW 10ᴛʜ Aᴠᴇɴᴜᴇ

Directions: Walk west on Burnside Street to NW 10th Avenue and take a right.
Continue north on 10th Avenue past Davis. Your destination will be on the right.

Mɪʟᴇꜱ: 0.4

LAST STOP

61 ILA UNION HALL
835 NW Eᴠᴇʀᴇᴛᴛ

Directions: Continue up 10th Avenue to Everett and take a right. Your
destination is one block ahead.

Mɪʟᴇꜱ: 0.07

To get back to your starting point, continue east on Everett Street for four-and-one-half blocks. To continue your Northwest Portland walking tour, go north on NW 9th Avenue and walk three blocks north to Hoyt Street. Go right past NW Park Avenue, then begin directions for Walking Tour Three (0.2 miles)

WALKING TOUR THREE: NORTHWEST
TOTAL SITES: 3 OR 4
TOTAL DISTANCE: 0.6 MILES, OR 1.7 MILES WITH OPTIONAL LAST SITE

STARTING POINT

122 SOUTHERN PACIFIC FREIGHT DEPOT

This site is on Hoyt Street between Broadway and Park Avenue.

FIRST STOP

106 GYPSY GATHERING PLACE PRIOR TO EXODUS

616 NW 10TH AVENUE

Directions: Walk west on Hoyt Street to 10th Avenue and take a right. Your destination will be on the right.

MILES: 0.2

SECOND/LAST STOP

61 OLD LOCAL 8 UNION HALL (CURRENTLY MCMENAMINS MISSION THEATRE)

1624 NW GLISAN STREET

Directions: Walk back (south) down NW 10th Avenue to Glisan Street and take a right. Continue west down Glisan Street past NW 16th Avenue. Your destination will be on the left.

MILES: 0.4

OPTIONAL LAST STOP

61 NEW LOCAL 8 UNION HALL

2435 NW FRONT AVENUE

Directions: Continue down Glisan Avenue to NW 17th Avenue and take a right. Walk one mile to Front Avenue and take a left. Your destination will be on the left.

MILES: 1.1

WALKING TOUR FOUR: INNER SOUTHWEST
TOTAL SITES: 8
TOTAL DISTANCE: 0.41 MILES

STARTING POINT

84 THE BOHEMIAN

910 SW WASHINGTON STREET

FIRST STOP

193 JORDAN, CAPLAN, PAUL, AND ETTER LAW FIRM

921 SW WASHINGTON STREET

Directions: Walk west on Washington less than a half block.

MILES: 0.01

SECOND STOP

 ## WOODMEN OF THE WORLD HALL
SW 11TH AVENUE AND ALDER STREET

Directions: Continue west on Washington. Take a left on SW 11th Avenue and continue until you reach Alder.

MILES: 0.1

THIRD STOP

 ## CITY CLUB OF PORTLAND AND GOVERNOR HOTEL
614 SW 11TH AVENUE

Directions: Continue south on SW 11th Avenue. The destination will be a half block down on your left.

MILES: 0.02

FOURTH STOP

SITE OF THE "DAUGHTERS OF AMERICA" BIRTHDAY CELEBRATION IN THE INTRODUCTION OF CHAPTER FOUR
721 SW 11TH AVENUE

Directions: Continue down SW 11th Avenue past Morrison. Your destination will be on the right.

MILES: 0.03

FIFTH STOP

 ## PORTLAND FORUM AT CENTRAL LIBRARY
1021 SW YAMHILL STREET

Directions: Continue south on 11th Avenue less than one block to Yamhill and take a left. Your destination will be on the right.

MILES: 0.06

SIXTH STOP

 ## WPA'S OREGON FEDERAL THEATER
914 SW 10TH AVENUE

Directions: Continue east on Yamhill and take your first right onto SW 10th Avenue. Your destination is a little over a block south on the left side.

MILES: 0.09

LAST STOP

ARLINGTON CLUB
811 SW SALMON STREET

Directions: Continue south on 10th Avenue less than a block to Salmon and take a left. Your destination is on the left.

MILES: 0.1

APPENDIX

RECOMMENDED PORTLAND HISTORIES

Readers of this guide will have no difficulty finding critical treatments of Portland's people and organizations in mainstream histories less receptive to radicals, Reds, suffragettes, civil rights militants, union organizers, and other dissenters. The books on this reading list offer fair portrayals of Portland's radical past.

Carl Abbott, *Portland: Gateway to the Northwest* (Northbridge, CA: American Historical Press, 1985).

Gordon DeMarco, *A Short History of Portland* (San Francisco: Lexikos, 1990).

Jewel Lansing, *Portland: People, Politics and Power, 1851–2001* (Corvallis, OR: Oregon State University Press, 2002).

E. Kimbark MacColl, *The Shaping of a City* (Portland, OR: Georgian Press, 1976).

E. Kimbark MacColl, *The Growth of a City* (Portland, OR: Georgian Press, 1979).

E. Kimbark MacColl (With Harry H. Stein), *Merchants, Money, and Power* (Portland, OR: Georgian Press, 1988).

Lewis L. McArthur, *Oregon Geographic Names* (4th ed.) (Portland, OR: Oregon Historical Society, 1974).

Elizabeth McLagan, *A Peculiar Paradise: A History of Blacks in Oregon, 1788–1940* (Portland, OR: Georgian Press, 1980).

Terence O'Donnell and Thomas Vaughan, *Portland: An Informal History and Guide* (Portland, OR: Western Imprints, 1984).

Eugene E. Snyder, *Portland Names and Neighborhoods* (Portland, OR: Binford and Mort Publishing, 1979).

John Trombold and Peter Donahue (Editors), *Reading Portland: The City in Prose* (Portland, OR: Oregon Historical Society, 2007).

FREQUENTLY USED ACRONYMS

American Civil Liberties Union ACLU
American Federation of Labor AFL
American Student Union ASU
Black Panther Party BPP
Communist Labor Party CLP
Congress of Industrial Organizations CIO
House Un-American Activities Committee HUAC
Industrial Workers of the World IWW
International Labor Defense ILD
International Longshore and Warehouse Union ILWU
International Longshoremen's Association ILA
International Woodworkers of America IWA
Joint Anti-Terrorism Task Force JTTF
National Association for the Advancement of Colored People NAACP
Northwest Liberation Front NLF
Northwest Tree Planters and Farm Workers United PCUN
Oregon Commonwealth Federation OCF
Oregon Workers Alliance OWA
Socialist Labor Party SLP
Students for a Democratic Society SDS
Subversive Activities Control Board SACB
Women's International League for Peace and Freedom WILPF
Works Progress Administration WPA

INDEX

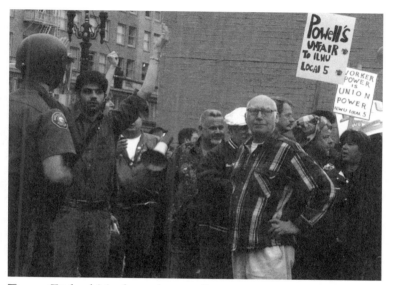

Michael Munk was born in Prague in 1934. He and his family moved to Portland to escape the Nazi occupation of Czechoslovakia in 1939. Munk received his bachelor's degree from Reed College, his master's in Political Science from the University of Oregon, and his doctorate in Politics from New York University. During his student years, he worked as a longshoreman on the Portland docks, sold tickets to summer concerts, and drove a truck during wheat harvests.

Munk's political activity began in the 1950s as a vocal opponent of nuclear testing. In 1959, he joined the US Army and served a term in South Korea. After serving in the military, he moved to New York where he was a national affairs editor for a leftist newsweekly, the *National Guardian*, until 1963. From 1970–1985, Munk taught political science at a number of universities, including the State University of New York at Stony Brook, Roosevelt University in Chicago, and Rutgers University in New Jersey.

He has since retired from teaching to live in Portland, Oregon where his interests and publications have focused on local radical history. In 2007, *The Oregonian* listed Munk among Portland's "local literary luminaries." He has been published in a number of magazines and had a monthly column called "Our Radical Past" in The Portland Alliance for several years. He continues to give voice to the stories history books ignore. Visit his website to discover more: www.michaelmunk.com.

OOLIGAN PRESS

Ooligan Press takes its name from a Native American word for the common smelt or candlefish. Ooligan is a general trade press rooted in the rich literary community of the Pacific Northwest and located in the Department of English at Portland State University. Ooligan is staffed by students pursuing master's degrees in an apprenticeship program under the guidance of a core faculty of publishing professionals.

PROJECT MANAGERS
Amanda Gomm
Kristin Howe
Shawnie Johnson
Anna Noak

EDITING MANAGERS
Julie Flanagan
Kenneth Hanour
Netanis Waters

EDITORS
Kathryn Banks
Leah Gibson-Blackfeather
Kate Savage
Chris Thomas
Lori Toner
Susan E. Wiget

PROOFREADERS
Kathryn Banks
Katelyn Benz
Cheryl Frey
Leah Gibson-Blackfeather
Ben Hamlin
Amanda Winterroth

INDEXER
Candice Peaslee

MARKETING MANAGERS
Bryan Coffelt
Dana Garbely
Candice Peaslee
Sara Simmonds

MARKETING TEAM
Cooper Lee Bombardier
Cheryl Frey
Laura Gleim
Kristin Howe
Shawnie Johnson
Sara Simmonds
Missy Ward
Amanda Winterroth

DESIGN MANAGERS
Kerri Higby
Rachel Moore

COVER DESIGN
Alan Dubinsky

INTERIOR DESIGN
Alan Dubinsky
Tristen Knight

DIGITAL DESIGN
Jesse Snavlin

COLOPHON

This second edition of *The Portland Red Guide* was set in two typefaces: the serif Goudy Oldstyle Std and the sans serif **Futura Std**.

Goudy Oldstyle Std is a digital version of the letters designed by Frederic W. Goudy in 1915 and was released by Adobe in 1985. We like its friendly feeling, and especially the upturned ear on the lowercase g.

Futura Std – Medium Condensed is used throughout the book – is based on the designs of Paul Renner from 1927. The geometric shapes of the letters are appealing and the wide range of weights makes the typeface versatile and adaptable.